Hedda Gabler

Crofts Classics

GENERAL EDITORS

Samuel H. Beer, *Harvard University*

O. B. Hardison, Jr., *The Folger Shakespeare Library*

HENRIK IBSEN

Hedda Gabler

TRANSLATED AND EDITED BY
Alan S. Downer

AHM Publishing Corporation
Arlington Heights, Illinois 60004

PRINTED IN THE UNITED STATES OF AMERICA

860

Fourteenth Printing

INTRODUCTION

❧

FOR HALF-A-CENTURY Henrik Ibsen has held a secure place in histories of the drama as the father of the modern theater, that is, as a reputation but no longer a vital force. Credit has been given to his rescue of the art from the sensationalism and sentimentality of popular melodrama, to his demonstration that the problems of contemporary society were legitimate subjects for serious dramatic treatment, to his innovations in the handling of exposition, characterization, and symbolism. His works were read and analyzed with appreciation as historical documents. But they appeared in their native habitat, the theater, only when some first-magnitude star sought a more modern vehicle than Shakespeare to display his (more often her) personality. To confine Ibsen to the study is to deny his genius as a playmaker, to make him a mere supporter of a star is to destroy the meticulous balance of his plays.

Recently there has been a stirring in the green room. A number of new translations have attempted to crack the marbled late-Victorian English of the authorized versions, which were true enough to the letter but rather remote from the spirit of Ibsen's style. The heavy burden of social significance imposed on the plays by their wily misinterpreter, Bernard Shaw, has been shifted to reveal the quintessential truths hidden by such catch phrases as "The New Woman" and "Anti-Idealism." And, most important, Ibsen has been redis-

covered as a man of the theater writing not for stars
but for audiences, and capable of speaking as directly
and as devastatingly to Americans in the middle of the
twentieth century as he had to Europeans at the end
of the nineteenth.

It is not surprising, on the one hand, that his con-
temporaries should have been blinded to Ibsen's ultimate intent by his apparent preoccupation with the
destruction of the individual by society. *A Doll's
House* (1879) depicts the revolt of a woman against
the inferior position decreed for her by nineteenth
century custom; in *Ghosts* (1881) a family is destroyed
by obedience to moribund convention; in *An Enemy of
the People* (1882) "the compact majority" is revealed
as reactionary, materialistic, and self-centered. Small
wonder that theatergoing members of the English compact majority rejected his work with jeers and epithets,
or that Shaw selected him as his own John the Baptist.
But Ibsen himself had declared:

All that I have written has not proceeded from a desire to
propagandize. I have been more the poet and less the social
philosopher than has been believed. I have never regarded
feminism as a question by itself, but as part of the question
of mankind. . . . *My task was the description of Man.*

Part of the reawakened interest in Ibsen among players
and playgoers has resulted from the discovery that he
was a true poet of the theater, something beyond a
poser of awkward questions, or a superb dramatic tech-
nician.

It is not surprising, on the other hand, that his con-
temporaries should have been blinded to his ultimate
achievement by this same technical skill. When he
chose to make the theater his career in 1851, he found
that the new plays being written were generally of
two types. There was the shapeless romantic historical
play, the enfeebled heir of the form best known from
the vivid, sweeping panoramic dramas of the great
Elizabethans, awkwardly cramped in the nineteenth

century by a production method which demanded the use of illusionistic scenery. And there was the tidy, economical, well-made play created to comply with both the new realistic stage settings and the increasing popular interest in scientific theories of cause and effect, but tricky in action, trivial in theme, and conventional in values and judgments. After experimenting with both forms, Ibsen developed a technique which, while completely natural in the drawing rooms and business offices of the realistic stage, recaptured the breadth and universality of the panoramic. Ibsen's *retrospective action* is, technically, a device for handling exposition, but it is of greater importance in characterization (the dramatic function of character) and theme.

In exposition the playwright informs his audience of what it must know about past events before it can follow and enjoy the action that the play is to unfold. On the sceneryless stage for which the panoramic drama was intended there was no material reason why the spectators could not be *shown* the earliest essential incidents of the story, or be informed of them directly by a character or commentator who made no pretense of being elsewhere than in the midst of his auditors. The development of realistic settings made the presentation of unlimited scenes impractical, and direct address to the audience illogical. Therefore the well-made play had to devise its own, not very satisfactory, expository technique; the job of filling in the audience was usually turned over to secondary characters who spent the best part of the first act informing each other of the things the audience had to know. If this was art, it made only a modest effort to conceal itself, and the exposition became more of a launching pad than an integral part of the total dramatic unit.

Ibsen assigns the exposition to principal, not secondary characters, and allows it to emerge gradually as the action develops instead of confining it to a first act ghetto. Superficially this is a gain in naturalness; the initial situation will often introduce major characters who have been long separated (the Tesmans are returning from a honeymoon trip) and must be brought up-to-date with each other's lives. But the delayed exposition also permits events from the past to be revealed at the moment when their relation to the present is most significant, most dramatic. Ibsen's typical structure, *retrospective action*, unfolding the past and the present simultaneously, thus becomes symbolic of one of his most characteristic themes, the tyranny of conventional moral and social concepts.

Such a tyranny is one of the forces that leads to the destruction of Hedda Gabler. The exposition constructs a carefully selective picture of her early environment and insists that certain inferences be drawn about her heredity. The title of the play emphasizes this aspect of the heroine's character and the problems that will confront her in the different social milieu into which she has married. But this is not the sole, or even the most important, concern of the work. "What I principally wanted," Ibsen wrote to his French translator, "was to depict human beings, human emotions, and human destinies, upon a groundwork of certain of the social conditions and principles of the present day."

With *Hedda Gabler* the whole direction of Ibsen's writing changes. While it is still realistic and contemporary, it does not require adaptation or rationalization to achieve universality. The characters speak Norwegian, but there is little mention of Norwegian places or customs. Significantly the setting is in "the west end of town," which for some inexplicable reason seems to be the better residential area of any community in the western world. And it is hardly necessary to see anything Norwegian in the ideals and customs of the military caste of which the Gablers are members. The frustrated, neurotic heroine, with no useful outlet for her talent and energy, has become the central figure of an international dramatic repertory since Ibsen, and has found explosive American treatment in the plays of Eugene O'Neill and Tennessee Williams. The issue of the play is not a problem posed for solution or a society brought to the bar of judgment. It is a tragedy of personalities in conflict, instinctively pursuing whatever goals their limited vision can perceive, always and forever alone, each the prisoner of his uniform of flesh. In *Hedda Gabler*, Ibsen for the first time achieves without compromise his task, the description of modern man.

The present translation is based on the first edition of the play, published in Copenhagen in December, 1890. Inevitably it has much in common with other English versions, but a particular effort has been made to avoid stage English, to preserve the colloquial speech rhythms, the characteristic vocabularies, the broken sentences by which Ibsen particularizes his characters. Tesman's fussy ejaculations, which are really verbalized question marks, reveal his character as much as does Brack's habitual assumption of the manner of a cross-examiner. Anyone fortunate enough to have seen Ibsen played on a Scandinavian stage will recognize the importance of his light, rapid, colloquial dialogue-style in de-emphasizing the merely theatrical in his work. But Ibsen was also a poet, and he delights in the finality of the poetic phrase ("with vine leaves in his hair") both to crystallize a moment, an emotion, or an idea, and to create dramatic irony when echoed or repeated. To appreciate more fully the effectiveness of this combination of colloquial and poetic rhythms and diction, it should (like any dialogue intended for the stage) be read aloud. It was never meant for the eye alone.

Hedda Gabler was first performed in Munich, 31 January 1891. In the following month it was produced in Berlin, Copenhagen, and Oslo, and in April in London with two American actresses, Elizabeth Robins and Marion Lea, in the principal roles. In the United States it has been played by Mrs. Fiske, Alla Nazimova, and Eva LeGallienne, among others, and rivals *A Doll's House* in world-wide popularity.

A.S.D.

HEDDA GABLER

THE CHARACTERS

JÖRGEN TESMAN, *research-fellow in cultural history*
HEDDA TESMAN, *his wife*
MISS JULIANE TESMAN, *his aunt*
MRS. ELVSTED
MR. BRACK, *an attorney and associate justice of the court*
EJLERT LÖVBORG
BERTE, *the Tesmans' maid*

The action takes place in Tesman's villa in the west end of town.

THE SCENE

A spacious, handsome, and tastefully furnished parlor, decorated in dark colors. At the back is a wide archway with curtains drawn apart. The archway leads into a smaller room decorated in the same style as the parlor. In the right wall of the front room is a folding door that leads out to the hall. Opposite, in the left wall, is a glass door, also with curtains drawn back. Through the panes can be seen the superstructure of a veranda outside and trees covered with autumn foliage. Well forward in the room, an oval table, with a cloth on it, surrounded by chairs. In front, by the wall on the right, a large, dark, porcelain stove, a high-backed armchair, a cushioned footrest and two small tables. Upper right, a corner sofa with a small round table before it. In front, on the left, a little way from the wall, a sofa. Above the glass door, a piano. On either side of the archway at the back a whatnot with terra-cotta and majolica ornaments. Against the back wall of the inner room a sofa, with a table and several chairs. Above the sofa hangs the portrait of a handsome elderly man in a General's uniform. A lamp with a milky glass shade hangs over the table. Arranged about the parlor are a number of bouquets in vases and glasses. The floors in both rooms are covered with thick carpets.

HEDDA GABLER

Act One

Morning light. Sun shines in through the glass door.
Miss Juliane Tesman, *wearing a hat and carrying
a parasol, comes in from the hall, followed by* Berte,
who carries a bouquet wrapped in paper. Miss Tesman *is a handsome, pleasant looking lady of about
65. She is attractively but simply dressed in grey.*
Berte *is a middle-aged woman, with a plain and
rather countrified look.*

Aunt Juliane (*steps inside the door, listens and
says softly*). Really, I don't believe they are stirring
yet!

Berte (*also softly*). Just what I told you, Miss Juliane.
Remember—the boat got in real late last night. And
after that! Lord—all the stuff the young mistress had
to unpack before she could get settled.

Aunt Juliane. Well, well—let them have their sleep.
But when they do come out they must have fresh
morning air.

She goes to the glass door and opens it wide.

1

BERTE (*by the table, not knowing what to do with the bouquet in her hand*). I swear there isn't a bit of space left. I think I'll put it here, Miss Juliane.

She places the bouquet on the piano.

AUNT JULIANE. Well now, you've got a new mistress, Berte. Goodness knows, I had a hard enough time bringing myself to let you go.

BERTE (*almost in tears*). And how about me, Miss Juliane? How can I tell you? After all those happy years I worked for you and Miss Rina.

AUNT JULIANE. We will just make the best of it, Berte. There was really nothing else to do. Jörgen must have you in his house, you know. He absolutely must. You've looked out for him ever since he was a little fellow.

BERTE. Yes, Miss Juliane, but I keep thinking of Miss Rina lying there at home. Poor thing—so helpless. And with only that new girl, too! Nothing in the world could teach that one to take care of a sick person.

AUNT JULIANE. Oh, I'll manage to train her. Anyway, I do most of the work myself, you know. You needn't be uneasy about my poor sister, Berte.

BERTE. Well, but there's something else, Miss Juliane. I'm really afraid I'll never be able to please the young mistress.

AUNT JULIANE. Well, for heaven's sake, there may be one or two things, at first.

BERTE. Because she's probably real fussy. . . .

AUNT JULIANE. Well, that's hardly surprising—General Gabler's daughter! Think of what she was used to having when her father was alive. Don't you remember her galloping down the road with the General? In that long black riding habit—with the plumes in her hat?

BERTE. Yes, indeed—I remember all right! But Good

Lord, I never would have thought in those days that she would pair off with Master Jörgen.

AUNT JULIANE. Neither did I. —But, that reminds me, Berte—from now on you mustn't say Master Jörgen. You must say Doctor Tesman.

BERTE. Yes, that was what the young mistress told me—last night—as soon as they came through the door. So it is really true, Miss Juliane.

AUNT JULIANE. Yes, it's really true. Just think, Berte—some foreign university has made him a doctor —while he was travelling, you know. I hadn't heard a word about it—until he told me himself on the pier.

BERTE. Well, he could be any thing he wanted to. A clever boy like him. But I never thought he planned to go around doctoring people.

AUNT JULIANE. No, no, he's not that kind of a doctor. (*Nods significantly.*) But, come to that, you may have to call him something even grander before long.

BERTE. Not really! What, for instance, Miss Juliane?

AUNT JULIANE (*smiling*). M'm—yes, you would like to know that!— (*With emotion.*) Ah, dear Lord— if poor Jochum could look up from his grave now and see what has happened to his little boy! (*Looks around.*) But, look here, Berte—why have you taken the slip covers off all the furniture?

BERTE. The mistress said I should do it. She can't stand slip covers on chairs, she says.

AUNT JULIANE. Do you suppose they will use this room—for everyday?

BERTE. Yes, that's what I understood. That is, from the mistress. Himself—the doctor—he said nothing.

JÖRGEN TESMAN *comes from the right into the back parlor, humming to himself, and carrying an empty suitcase. He is a middle-sized, young-looking man of 33, rather stout, with an open,*

*round, cheerful face, blond hair and beard. He
wears glasses and is dressed in a comfortable,
rather slipshod suit.*

AUNT JULIANE. Good morning, good morning, Jörgen.

TESMAN (*in the archway between the two rooms*).
Aunt Julle! Dear Aunt Julle! (*Goes to her and shakes
hands warmly.*) Way out here—so early in morning!
What—?

AUNT JULIANE. Why, I should think you could guess
that I just had to see how you are getting along.

TESMAN. Even though you didn't get a proper night's
rest?

AUNT JULIANE. Oh, that doesn't matter at all.

TESMAN. You got home from the pier all right? Yes?

AUNT JULIANE. Yes, quite all right—thank goodness.
Mr. Brack was so kind. He took me right to my door.

TESMAN. We were so sorry we couldn't take you in
our carriage. But you could see for yourself—Hedda
had so much luggage to bring along with her.

AUNT JULIANE. Yes, she certainly had plenty of boxes.

BERTE (*to* TESMAN). Shall I go in and ask the
mistress if there's anything I can give her a hand with?

TESMAN. No thank you, Berte—you needn't do that.
If she wants anything she will ring, she said.

BERTE (*going towards the right*). Very well.

TESMAN. But, look here, though—take this bag with
you.

BERTE (*taking it*). I'll put it up in the attic.

She goes out by the hall door.

TESMAN. Just think, Aunt Julle, the whole of that
bag was stuffed full of notes I copied. You wouldn't
believe how much I picked up going through the
archives—wonderful old details that no one knew
anything about—

AUNT JULIANE. Yes, you certainly didn't waste any time on your honeymoon, Jörgen.

TESMAN. No, I certainly did not. But take off your hat, Aunt Julle. Look here! Let me unfasten the strings. —All right?

AUNT JULIANE (*while he does so*). Bless me—this is just like having you still at home with us.

TESMAN (*looking at the hat in his hands*). Why, what a fine, stylish hat you've treated yourself to!

AUNT JULIANE. I bought it for Hedda's sake.

TESMAN. For Hedda's sake? How's that?

AUNT JULIANE. Yes, so that Hedda wouldn't be ashamed of me if we happened to walk down the street together.

TESMAN (*patting her cheek*). You always think of everything, Aunt Julle. (*Puts the hat on the table.*) And now, look here—let's make ourselves comfortable on the sofa. And chat a little, till Hedda comes in.

They seat themselves. She stands her parasol against the corner of the sofa.

AUNT JULIANE (*takes both his hands and looks at him*). How good it is to have you before my very eyes, Jörgen, large as life! Ah, you—poor Jochum's own boy!

TESMAN. And for me, too! To see you again, Aunt Julle! You, who took the place of father and mother both, to me.

AUNT JULIANE. Yes, I know you will always keep a place in your heart for your old aunts.

TESMAN. I take it there is no improvement in Aunt Rina. Right?

AUNT JULIANE. Well, no, you—there is really no improvement possible for her, poor thing. She lies there, just the way she has been all these years. But heaven grant she'll stay with me a while yet. Without her,

I don't know what I'd do with my life. Especially now I don't have you to look out for any more.

TESMAN (*patting her shoulder*). There, there, there—!

AUNT JULIANE (*suddenly changing her tone*). No, but to think that you are a married man, Jörgen!—— And that it was you that carried off Hedda Gabler. The lively Hedda Gabler! Think of it—she, who always had so many suitors around her!

TESMAN (*hums a little and smiles complacently*). Yes, I honestly believe I have certain good friends here who walk about the town and envy me.

AUNT JULIANE. And this fine long wedding trip you've had! More than five—almost six months—

TESMAN. Well, it was a sort of research tour for me, too. What with the archives that I had to consult. And I had to read so many books, too, you know.

AUNT JULIANE. Yes, I suppose so. (*More confidentially, and lowering her voice a little.*) But look here, Jörgen, have you nothing, you know, special to tell me?

TESMAN. About the trip?

AUNT JULIANE. Yes.

TESMAN. No, there is nothing I haven't written you in my letters. I took a doctorate down there—but I told you that last night.

AUNT JULIANE. Yes, that sort of thing, yes. But I mean—haven't you any—any—hopes—?

TESMAN. Hopes?

AUNT JULIANE. Good Lord, Jörgen—I'm your old auntie!

TESMAN. Why, of course I have hopes, yes.

AUNT JULIANE. So!

TESMAN. I have the very best hopes of getting a professorship one of these days.

AUNT JULIANE. Oh, a professorship, yes—

TESMAN. Indeed, I think I may say there is a certainty of my getting it. But my dear Aunt Julle— you know that perfectly well yourself!

AUNT JULIANE (*laughing to herself*). Yes, of course I do. You are quite right there. (*Changing the subject.*) But we were talking about your trip. It must have cost a pretty penny, Jörgen?

TESMAN. Well, you see—that generous travelling-fellowship helped a good bit of the way.

AUNT JULIANE. But I can't understand how you stretched it to pay for two.

TESMAN. No, that's not so easy to understand—eh?

AUNT JULIANE. And especially when you were travel-ing with a lady. —That makes it ever so much more expensive, I've heard tell.

TESMAN. Yes, that is true—it does make it a little more expensive. But Hedda *had* to have this trip, Aunt Julle! She really *had* to have it. Nothing else would do.

AUNT JULIANE. No, no, I suppose not. A honeymoon abroad seems to be quite indispensable nowadays. —But tell me now—have you had a chance to look the house over yet?

TESMAN. Yes, I certainly have! I have been explor-ing ever since daylight.

AUNT JULIANE. And what do you think of it, all in all? *JÖRGEN NAIVE*

TESMAN. Excellent! Quite excellent! Only I can't imagine what we will do with the two empty rooms between the back parlor, there, and Hedda's bedroom.

AUNT JULIANE (*laughing*). Oh, my dear Jörgen, I expect you'll find some use for them as time goes on.

TESMAN. Yes, of course, you are quite right, Aunt Julle! You mean as I build up my library, don't you?

AUNT JULIANE. Quite so, my dear boy. I was thinking of your library.

TESMAN. I am specially glad for Hedda's sake.

Before we were engaged, she often said she would
never really want to live anywhere but in the widow
Falk's villa.

AUNT JULIANE. Yes, just think—what a coincidence
that Mrs. Falk's house should come on the market.
Just after you had started on your trip.

TESMAN. Yes, Aunt Julle. We had luck on our side,
didn't we?

AUNT JULIANE. But so expensive, my dear Jörgen!
It will be very expensive for you—keeping this big
place up.

TESMAN (*looks at her, a little crestfallen*). Yes, it
probably will be, won't it, Aunt Julle?

AUNT JULIANE. My goodness, yes.

TESMAN. How much do you think? Approximately—
what?

AUNT JULIANE. Oh, I can't possibly guess until all
the bills come in.

TESMAN. Well, fortunately, Mr. Brack, being a
lawyer, arranged the easiest possible terms for me.
He said so himself in a letter he wrote to Hedda.

AUNT JULIANE. Yes, don't you worry about it, my
dear boy. —And as for the furniture and all the
carpeting, I have given security for them.

TESMAN. Security? You? My dear Aunt Julle—what
sort of security could *you* give?

AUNT JULIANE. I have taken a mortgage on our
annuity.

TESMAN (*jumping up*). What! On the annuity—yours
and Aunt Rina's?

AUNT JULIANE. Yes, I didn't know of any other way,
you see.

TESMAN (*standing in front of her*). Have you taken
leave of your senses, Aunt Julle! Your annuity—that's
the only thing you and Aunt Rina have to live on.

AUNT JULIANE. Now, now, don't take on so about it. It's only a formality, you know. That's what Mr. Brack told me. He was the one who was kind enough to arrange the whole business for me. Just a formality, he said.

TESMAN. Yes, it may very well be. But just the same—

AUNT JULIANE. Because now you will have your own salary to depend on! And, Good Heavens, what if we did have to pay a little out—! To help out a bit at the start—! Why that would be a real pleasure to us.

TESMAN. Oh, Aunt Julle—will you never get tired of making sacrifices for me?

AUNT JULIANE (*rising and putting her hands on his shoulders*). Have I any other happiness in this world except to smooth your way for you, my dear boy? You, who haven't had a father or mother to help you. And now we have reached the goal, Jörgen. Sometimes things looked pretty black for us, but, God be praised, you've reached the top.

TESMAN. Yes, it really is wonderful how everything has worked out.

AUNT JULIANE. Yes. —And those who opposed you— those who wanted to bar the way against you—now you have them at your feet. They have fallen, Jörgen. The one who was your most dangerous rival—his fall was the worst. —And now he lies on the bed he has made for himself—poor misguided creature.

TESMAN. Have you heard anything of Ejlert? Since I went away, I mean?

AUNT JULIANE. Nothing except that they say he has written a new book.

TESMAN. What did you say! Ejlert Lövborg! Recently —you mean?

AUNT JULIANE. Yes, so they say. Heaven knows

whether there can be much good in it. Ah, when *your* new book comes out—that will be something else again, Jörgen! What is it to be about?

TESMAN. It will deal with the domestic crafts of Brabant during the Middle Ages.

AUNT JULIANE. Just think—to be able to write about such things as that!

TESMAN. It may be some time before the book is finished. I have all that great mass of notes to arrange first, you know.

AUNT JULIANE. Yes, collecting and arranging—no one can beat you at that. In that you are my poor Jochum's own son.

TESMAN. It will be a pleasure to get to work at it. Especially now that I have my own comfortable home to work in.

AUNT JULIANE. And, more important, now that you have got the wife your heart was set on, Jörgen dear.

TESMAN (*embracing her*). Oh, yes, yes, Aunt Julle. Hedda—that is the nicest part of it all! (*Looks towards the archway.*) I think she's coming—eh?

HEDDA *enters from the left through the back parlor. She is a woman of 29. Her face and figure show good breeding and distinction. Her complexion is pale and opaque. Her steel grey eyes express a cold, unruffled calm. Her hair is an agreeable light brown, but not particularly thick. She is dressed in a stylish, loose-fitting gown.*

AUNT JULIANE (*going to meet Hedda*). Good morning, my dear Hedda, a very good morning.

HEDDA (*holds out her hand*). Good morning, Miss Tesman! Such an early call, how friendly.

AUNT JULIANE (*showing some embarrassment*). Well, did the bride sleep well in her new home?

HEDDA. Oh yes, thanks. Pretty well.

TESMAN (*laughing*). Pretty well! Now that's a good one, Hedda! You were sleeping like a rock when I got up.

HEDDA. Fortunately. Of course one always has to get used to anything new, Miss Tesman. Little by little. (*Looking toward the left.*) Oh—there, the maid has left the veranda door open and let in a whole flood of sunshine.

AUNT JULIANE (*going toward the door*). Well, then, we'll just shut it.

HEDDA. No, no, not that! Dear Tesman, draw the curtains together. That will give a softer light.

TESMAN (*at the door*). All right—all right. See there—Hedda, now you have both shade and fresh air.

HEDDA. Yes, we certainly must have fresh air. All these blessed flowers. —But—won't you sit down, Miss Tesman?

AUNT JULIANE. No, thank you. Now I have seen that everything is all right here—thank heaven! —I must see about getting home again, to my sister who is lying there with nothing to do but wait for me, poor thing.

TESMAN. Please give her my very best love, and say I will come over to see her later today.

AUNT JULIANE. Yes, yes, I'll be sure to tell her. But by-the-bye, Jörgen—(*feeling in her dress pocket*)— I had almost forgot—I have something here for you.

TESMAN. What is it, Aunt Julle? Eh?

AUNT JULIANE (*produces a flat parcel wrapped in newspaper and hands it to him*). Look, my dear boy.

TESMAN (*opening the parcel*). Well, Good Lord! —You really saved them for me, Aunt Julle! Hedda! Isn't this touching—eh?

HEDDA (*beside the whatnot on the right*). Yes, dear. What is it?

TESMAN. My old morning shoes! My slippers, see!

HEDDA. Oh, yes. I remember you talked about them all the time while we were traveling.

TESMAN. Yes, I missed them so much. (*Goes up to her.*) Now you shall see them, Hedda!

HEDDA (*going towards the stove*). Thank you, I'm really not very interested.

TESMAN (*following her*). Just think—Aunt Rina embroidered these for me, sick as she was. Oh you can't think how many memories cluster around them.

insensitivity

HEDDA (*at the table*). Scarcely for me.

AUNT JULIANE. Hedda is right about that, Jörgen.

TESMAN. Well, but I thought that now she belongs to the family—

HEDDA (*interrupting*). We shall never be able to manage with this maid, Tesman.

AUNT JULIANE. Not manage with Berte?

TESMAN. What makes you say *that*, dear? Eh?

HEDDA (*pointing*). Look at that! She has left her old hat behind her on the table.

TESMAN (*dismayed, drops the slippers on the floor*) Why Hedda—

cruelty

HEDDA. Imagine—if someone should come in and see it!

TESMAN. But Hedda—that's Aunt Julle's hat.

HEDDA. It is?

AUNT JULIANE (*taking it up*). Yes indeed it's mine. And what's more it's not old, Hedda dear.

HEDDA. I really did not look at it closely, Miss Tesman.

AUNT JULIANE (*putting on the hat*). The truth of the matter is, it's the first time I have worn it. Absolutely the first time.

TESMAN. And it's a very nice hat, too—really fine!

AUNT JULIANE. Oh, it's not all that, Jörgen. (*Looks around her.*) My parasol—? Ah, here. (*Takes it.*) For this is mine too—(*mutters*) not Berte's.

TESMAN. A new hat and a new parasol! Just think, Hedda!

HEDDA. It's very nice—charming.

TESMAN. Yes, isn't it? Eh? But Aunt Julle, take a good look at Hedda before you go! See how nice and charming *she* is!

AUNT JULIANE. Oh, my dear boy, that's nothing new. Hedda has been lovely all her life.

She nods and goes towards the right.

TESMAN (*following*). Yes, but have you noticed how plump and glowing she is? How she has filled out during our trip?

HEDDA (*crossing the room*). Oh, never mind that—!

AUNT JULIANE (*who has stopped and turned around*). Filled out?

TESMAN. Yes, Aunt Julle. Of course you can't see it so well now that she has that dress on. But I, who have had the opportunity of—

HEDDA (*at the glass door, impatiently*). Oh, you didn't have an opportunity for anything.

TESMAN. It must have been the mountain air in the Tyrol—

HEDDA (*curtly*). I am exactly the same as I was when I started.

TESMAN. Yes, so you say. But you certainly aren't. Don't you agree with me, Aunt Julle?

AUNT JULIANE (*gazing at her with folded hands*). Hedda is lovely—lovely—lovely. (*Goes up to her, takes her head between both hands, draws it downwards and kisses her hair.*) God bless and preserve Hedda Tesman —for Jörgen's sake.

HEDDA (*gently freeing herself*). Oh—! Let me go.

AUNT JULIANE (*with quiet emotion*). I shall come to see you two every single day.

TESMAN. Yes, you will do that, won't you, Aunt Julle? Eh?

AUNT JULIANE. Good-bye—good-bye!

She goes out by the hall door with TESMAN, *leaving the door open.* TESMAN *can be heard repeating his message to Aunt Rina and his thanks for the slippers.*

In the meantime, HEDDA *crosses the room, raising her arms and clenching her hands as if in desperation. Then she flings back the curtains from the glass door and stands looking out.*

A moment later, TESMAN *returns, closing the hall door behind him.*

TESMAN (*picks up the slippers from the floor*). What are you staring at, Hedda?

HEDDA (*more calm and controlled*). I am looking at the leaves. They are so yellow. And so withered.

TESMAN (*wraps up the slippers and puts them on the table*). After all, we are well into September now.

HEDDA (*restless again*). Yes, imagine! We are already in—in September.

TESMAN. Don't you think Aunt Julle's manner was strange, dear? Almost formal? Can you think what was the matter with her? Eh?

HEDDA. I hardly know her, you see. Doesn't she usually act that way?

TESMAN. No, not as she was today.

HEDDA (*coming away from the door*). Do you think she was upset about the hat?

TESMAN. Oh, not much. Perhaps a little, just at the moment—

HEDDA. But what a way to behave, to throw her hat

just anywhere in the parlor. <u>One does not do that sort of thing.</u> SOCIAL ACCEPTABILITY, CONVENTION

TESMAN. Well, you can be sure Aunt Julle won't do it again.

HEDDA. In any case, I'll make it up with her.

TESMAN. Yes, my dear, good Hedda, if you only will.

HEDDA. When you go to see them later today, you might ask her over for the evening.

TESMAN. Yes, I'll do that. And there's one thing more you could do that would please her very much.

HEDDA. What?

TESMAN. If you could only bring yourself to be a little less distant with her. For my sake, Hedda? Eh?

HEDDA. No, no Tesman—you must not expect me to do that. I have told you that before. I shall try to call her "Aunt" and you must be satisfied with that.   SNOBBY

TESMAN. Well, well, then. Only I think now that you belong to the family—

HEDDA. M'm—I really don't see why—

She goes up towards the archway.

TESMAN (*after a pause*). Is something the matter, Hedda? Eh?

HEDDA. I'm just looking at my old piano. It doesn't go at all well with these other things.

TESMAN. The first time I draw my salary, we'll see about exchanging it.

HEDDA. No, no—no exchanging. I don't want to part with it. We can put it there in the back room. And then we can get another here in its place. When it's convenient, I mean.

TESMAN (*a little taken aback*). Yes—of course we could do that.

HEDDA (*takes up the bouquet from the piano*). These flowers weren't here last night when we arrived.

TESMAN. Aunt Julle must have brought them for you.

HEDDA (*examining the bouquet*). A calling card. (*Reads:*) "Shall return later in the day." Can you guess who it is from?

TESMAN. No. Who is it? Eh?

HEDDA. It says "Mrs. Elvsted."

TESMAN. Not really? Sheriff Elvsted's wife? Who used to be Miss Rysing?

JEALOUS

HEDDA. Exactly. The girl with the irritating hair that she was always showing off. Your old flame, I've been told.

TESMAN (*laughing*). Oh, that didn't last long; and it was before I knew you, Hedda. But imagine—her being in town.

HEDDA. Strange that she should call on us. I have hardly heard a thing about her since we were at school together.

TESMAN. Yes, I haven't seen her either for heaven knows how long. I wonder how she can stand living in such an out-of-the-way hole—eh?

HEDDA (*thinks a moment and speaks suddenly*). Listen, Tesman—isn't it somewhere up in that district that he—that Ejlert Lövborg is living?

TESMAN. Yes, he is somewhere in that part of the country.

BERTE *enters by the hall door.*

BERTE. Ma'am, she's here again, the lady that brought some flowers a little while ago (*pointing*). The flowers you have in your hand, ma'am.

HEDDA. Ah, is she? Well, show her in, please.

BERTE *opens the door for* MRS. ELVSTED *and goes out herself.* MRS. ELVSTED *is a fragile woman, with pretty, soft features. Her eyes are light blue, large, round and somewhat prominent with a startled, inquiring look. Her hair is almost flaxen, and unusually thick and wavy. She is a few years younger than* HEDDA. *Her dress is dark colored, tasteful, but not quite in the latest fashion.*

HEDDA (*warmly*). How do you do, my dear Mrs. Elvsted? How nice to see you again.

MRS. ELVSTED (*nervously, trying to control herself*). Yes, it's a very long time since we met.

TESMAN (*giving her his hand*). And we, too—eh?

HEDDA. Thank you for your lovely flowers—

MRS. ELVSTED. Oh, please—! I'd have come directly here yesterday afternoon, but I heard that you were traveling—

TESMAN. Have you just come to town? Eh?

MRS. ELVSTED. I got here yesterday noon. Oh I was almost desperate when I heard you were not home.

HEDDA. Desperate! Why?

TESMAN. But my dear, dear Mrs. Rysing—Mrs. Elvsted, I mean to say—

HEDDA. I hope that nothing is the matter.

MRS. ELVSTED. Yes, it is. I don't know another living soul here I can turn to.

HEDDA (*laying the bouquet on the table*). Come—let's sit here on the sofa—

MRS. ELVSTED. Oh, I am too nervous to sit down.

HEDDA. Oh, no, you're not. Come here.

She draws MRS. ELVSTED *down on the sofa and sits at her side.*

TESMAN. Now, what is it, Mrs. Elvsted?

HEDDA. Has something particular gone wrong up there where you live?

MRS. ELVSTED. Yes—that is, yes and no. Oh—I do hope you won't misunderstand me—

HEDDA. Perhaps it would be best to tell us the whole story, Mrs. Elvsted.

TESMAN. That's the reason you have come—isn't it?

MRS. ELVSTED. Yes, yes—of course it is. Well, then, first I must tell you—if you don't know already—that Ejlert Lövborg also is here in town.

HEDDA. Is Lövborg—!

TESMAN. No! Has Ejlert Lövborg come back again? Think of that, Hedda!

HEDDA. Good heavens, I heard what she said.

MRS. ELVSTED. He has been here a week now. Think of it—a whole week! In this dangerous city. Alone! With all the evil company he could find here.

HEDDA. But my dear Mrs. Elvsted—what has *he* to do with you particularly?

MRS. ELVSTED (*with a frightened glance—rapidly*). He was the tutor for the children.

HEDDA. For your children?

MRS. ELVSTED. For my husband's. I have no children.

HEDDA. For your step-children, then.

MRS. ELVSTED. Yes.

TESMAN (*hesitantly*) But was he—I don't know how to put it—was he—regular enough in his habits to fill such a post? Eh?

MRS. ELVSTED. For the last two years no one could say a word against him.

TESMAN. Not really? Think of that, Hedda!

HEDDA. I heard.

MRS. ELVSTED. Not the slightest word, I assure you! About anything. But just the same——now that I know he is here—in this great city—and with a good deal of money in his hands. Well, I am worried to death about him.

TESMAN. Why didn't he stay up there where he was? With you and your husband? Eh?

MRS. ELVSTED. After his book came out he was too restless and excited to stay up there with us.

TESMAN. Oh, that's right—Aunt Julle said he had published a new book.

MRS. ELVSTED. Yes, a big new book, dealing with cultural history—a kind of survey. It's been out about two
weeks. And it has been bought and read so widely—
and made such a great sensation—

TESMAN. Has it really? Then it must be something he
wrote during his better days.

MRS. ELVSTED. Long ago, you mean?

TESMAN. Yes, exactly.

MRS. ELVSTED. No, he wrote it all while he was up
there with us. —Recently—within the last year.

TESMAN. Isn't that good to hear, Hedda! Think of
that.

MRS. ELVSTED. Ah, yes, if he will only keep it up!

HEDDA. Have you met him here in town?

MRS. ELVSTED. No, not yet. I had so much trouble
finding his address. But just this morning I finally discovered it.

HEDDA (*looks closely at her*). Do you know, it seems
a little strange to me that your husband—mm—

MRS. ELVSTED (*with a nervous start*). That my husband! What?

HEDDA. That he should send *you* to town on such a
mission. That he didn't come here himself and look
after his friend.

MRS. ELVSTED. Oh, no, no—my husband wouldn't
have time for that. Also it happened that there was—
some shopping I had to do.

HEDDA (*smiling slightly*). Ah, that is a different matter, then.

MRS. ELVSTED (*rising quickly and uneasily*). And
now I beg you, implore you, Mr. Tesman—be kind to
Ejlert Lövborg if he comes to you! And he's sure to do
that. You see, you were such good friends in the old

days. And you are both working in the same field. The same specialty—as far as I can understand.

TESMAN. We were once, anyway.

MRS. ELVSTED. Yes, that is why I ask so earnestly that you—that you, too, keep a watchful eye on him. Oh, you will promise me that, Mr. Tesman—won't you?

TESMAN. Yes, with the greatest pleasure, Mrs. Rysing—

HEDDA. Elvsted.

TESMAN. I assure you I will do everything in my power for Ejlert. You rely on me.

MRS. ELVSTED. Oh how very, very kind of you! (*Pressing his hands.*) Thank you, thank you, thank you! (*Frightened.*) You see, my husband thinks so highly of him!

HEDDA (*rising*). You ought to write to him, Tesman. Perhaps he may not come to see you of his own accord.

TESMAN. Well, I dare say that would be the right thing to do, Hedda? Eh?

HEDDA. And the sooner the better. Right now, I would think.

MRS. ELVSTED (*imploringly*). Oh, if only you would.

TESMAN. I'll do it right now. Do you have his address, Mrs.—Mrs. Elvsted?

MRS. ELVSTED. Yes. (*Gives him a slip of paper from her pocket.*) Here it is.

TESMAN. Good, good. Then I'll go in— (*Looks around.*) That reminds me—my slippers? Oh, here.

Takes them up from the table and starts off.

HEDDA. Now write a warm friendly letter to him. And a good long one, too.

TESMAN. Yes, certainly.

MRS. ELVSTED. But please don't mention that I asked you to do it.

TESMAN. No, that is quite understood. Eh?

He goes out to the right, through the back parlor.

HEDDA (*goes up to* MRS. ELVSTED, *smiles, and speaks softly*). Now see! We have killed two flies with one slap.

MRS. ELVSTED. What do you mean?

HEDDA. Didn't you understand that I wanted him to leave us?

MRS. ELVSTED. Yes, to write the letter—

HEDDA. But also so that I might speak to you alone.

MRS. ELVSTED (*confused*). About the same thing?

HEDDA. Precisely. About that.

MRS. ELVSTED (*alarmed*). But there is nothing more, Mrs. Tesman! Absolutely nothing more!

HEDDA. Oh yes, but there is. There is quite a lot more. That much I can understand. Come here—we'll sit down and be cosy and confidential.

She forces MRS. ELVSTED *into the easy chair beside the stove and seats herself on one of the footstools.*

MRS. ELVSTED (*anxiously, with a glance at her watch*). But my dear Mrs. Tesman. —I was just thinking that I must be going.

HEDDA. Oh, you can't be in such a hurry. —Now, tell me a little about what your life is like at home.

MRS. ELVSTED. Oh, that's the very last thing I want to talk about.

HEDDA. But to me, dear—? Why, Good Lord, we went to the same school.

MRS. ELVSTED. Yes, but you were in the class ahead of me. Oh, how frightened I was of you in those days!

HEDDA. You were afraid of me?

MRS. ELVSTED. Yes, dreadfully afraid. Because when we met on the stairs you always used to pull my hair.

HEDDA. No, did I do *that?*

MRS. ELVSTED. Yes, and one time you said you would burn it off.

HEDDA. Oh that was just talk. You can see that.

MRS. ELVSTED. Yes, but I was so stupid in those days. —And after that—we drifted so far—so far apart from each other. Our worlds were so entirely different.

HEDDA. Well, then, we'll see if we can drift together again. Now listen to me. At school we were very informal. And we called each other by our first names—

MRS. ELVSTED. No. You're wrong about that.

HEDDA. No, not at all! I remember very well. So now we are going to be confidential, just as in the old days. (*Draws the stool nearer to* MRS. ELVSTED.) There now! (*Kisses her cheek.*) You must drop the formality and call me Hedda.

MRS. ELVSTED (*pressing and patting her hands*). Oh, so much goodness and kindness! That is something I am not used to.

HEDDA. There, there, there! And I shall treat you like a friend, as in the old days, and call you my dear Thora.

MRS. ELVSTED. My name is Thea.

HEDDA. Of course. Of course, I meant Thea. (*With a compassionate glance.*) So you are not used to goodness and kindness, Thea? Not in your own home?

MRS. ELVSTED. Oh, if I only had a home! But I haven't one. I've never had a home.

HEDDA (*with a long look at her*). I guessed it might be something like that.

MRS. ELVSTED (*staring helplessly before her*). Yes—yes—yes.

HEDDA. I don't quite remember now. But didn't you first go up to the Sheriff's as his housekeeper?

MRS. ELVSTED. I was really supposed to be a governess. But his wife—his late wife—she was an invalid,

—and was bedridden most of the time. So I had to take charge of the housework as well.

HEDDA. But then—in the end—you became mistress of the house.

MRS. ELVSTED (*gloomily*). Yes, I did.

HEDDA. Let me see—about how long ago was that?

MRS. ELVSTED. That I was married?

HEDDA. Yes.

MRS. ELVSTED. Five years ago, now.

HEDDA. To be sure; it must be that.

MRS. ELVSTED. Oh, those five years—! Or at least the last two or three! Oh, Mrs. Tesman, if you could only imagine—

HEDDA (*giving her a little slap on the hand*). Mrs. Tesman? Tut, Thea!

MRS. ELVSTED. Yes, yes I will try. —Well, if—you could only guess, and understand—

HEDDA (*lightly*). Ejlert Lövborg has also been up there about three years, I believe?

MRS. ELVSTED (*with a doubting look*). Ejlert Lövborg? Yes—he has.

HEDDA. Did you know him before that, when you were here in town?

MRS. ELVSTED. Hardly at all. That is to say—I knew him by name, of course.

HEDDA. But up there—he came to your house?

MRS. ELVSTED. Yes, he came over to the farm every day. You see, he gave lessons to the children. Because it turned out I couldn't manage them with everything else.

HEDDA. Of course, that's very understandable. —And your husband—? I suppose he was often away from home?

MRS. ELVSTED. Yes. You see, Mrs.—Hedda, the Sheriff has to travel about the district a good deal.

HEDDA (*leaning against the chair arm*). Thea—my poor, sweet Thea—now you must tell me everything—exactly what it is like.

MRS. ELVSTED. Well, then, you'll have to ask me questions.

HEDDA. What sort of a man is your husband, Thea? I mean—you know—in family matters? Is he kind to you?

MRS. ELVSTED (*evasively*). He is quite sure that he does everything for the best.

HEDDA. I should think he must be rather old for you. About twenty years older?

MRS. ELVSTED (*with irritation*). Yes, there is that, too. That and other things. Everything about him is objectionable! We have not an idea in common. Not a thing in the world—he and I.

HEDDA. But doesn't he love you, just the same? In his own way?

MRS. ELVSTED. Oh, I don't know what he feels. I think I'm just useful to him. And it doesn't cost him much to keep me. I'm a bargain.

HEDDA. That is stupid of you.

MRS. ELVSTED (*shaking her head*). It can't be any other way. Not with him. I don't think he really cares for anyone but himself. And perhaps a little for the children.

HEDDA. And for Ejlert Lövborg, Thea.

MRS. ELVSTED (*looking at her*). For Ejlert Lövborg? Whatever makes you think that?

HEDDA. But my dear—I should think when he sends you all the way to town after him— (*With an almost imperceptible smile.*) And besides you said so yourself, to Tesman.

MRS. ELVSTED (*with a little nervous twitch*). Did I? Yes, so I did. (*Vehemently, but not loudly.*) No—I may just as well tell you first as last! For it will all come out into the daylight eventually.

HEDDA. Why, my dear Thea—?

MRS. ELVSTED. Well, it is best to be short and sweet then. My husband did not know I was coming.

HEDDA. What! Your husband, didn't know it!

MRS. ELVSTED. No, of course not. As a matter of fact, he was away from home. He was traveling himself. Oh, I couldn't stand it any longer, Hedda! It was absolutely impossible! I should have been utterly alone up there in the future.

HEDDA. Well? And then?

MRS. ELVSTED. So I packed up some of my things, you understand. Just the necessities. Quietly as I could. And then I left the farm.

HEDDA. Without a word?

MRS. ELVSTED. Yes—and took the train straight to town.

HEDDA. Why, my dear, good Thea—that you should dare to do that!

MRS. ELVSTED (*rising and crossing the room*). Yes, but what else in the world could I do?

HEDDA. But what do you think your husband will say when you go back home?

MRS. ELVSTED (*at the table, looks at her*). Back up there to *him?*

HEDDA. Yes. What—what?

MRS. ELVSTED. I will never go back up there to him.

HEDDA (*rising and going towards her*). Then you have left your home—for good and all?

MRS. ELVSTED. Yes. I couldn't think of anything else to do.

HEDDA. And then—you did it so openly.

MRS. ELVSTED. Oh, such things can't be kept secret, anyway.

HEDDA. But what do you think people will say about you, Thea?

MRS. ELVSTED. God knows they will say what they will. (*Sits wearily and sadly on the sofa.*) Because I haven't done anything but what I had to do.

A short silence.

HEDDA. What do you think you will do now? How will you live?

MRS. ELVSTED. That I don't know yet. I only know this, I *must* live here, where Ejlert Lövborg is—if I am to go on living at all.

HEDDA (*takes a chair from the table, sits beside her and caresses her hands*). My dear Thea—how did this happen—this friendship between you and Ejlert Lövborg?

MRS. ELVSTED. Oh, somehow it happened little by little. I came to have a kind of influence over him.

HEDDA. So?

MRS. ELVSTED. He gave up his old habits. Not because I asked him to. I never dared do that. But he noticed of course that they were distasteful to me. And so he quit them.

HEDDA (*concealing an involuntary sneer*). Then you have reformed him—as people say—you, my little Thea.

MRS. ELVSTED. Yes, he says so himself, anyway. And he, for his part—he has made a real human being of me. Taught me to think—and to understand one thing after another.

HEDDA. I take it that he tutored *you*, also?

MRS. ELVSTED. No, not exactly tutored. But he talked to me. Talked about such an endless number of things. And then came the lovely, happy time when I began to share his work! He let me help him!

HEDDA. Oh, you did?

MRS. ELVSTED. Yes! Whenever he wrote anything I had to be present.

HEDDA. Like two good comrades in fact?

MRS. ELVSTED (*eagerly*). Comrades! Yes, just think, Hedda—he called it that, too!— Oh, I ought to feel completely happy. But I can't, not completely. For I don't know how long it will last.

HEDDA. Are you no surer of him than that?

MRS. ELVSTED (*gloomily*). A woman's shadow stands between Ejlert Lövborg and me.

HEDDA (*with an anxious look at her*). Who can *that* be?

MRS. ELVSTED. I don't know. Some one from his— from his past. Some one he has never completely forgotten.

HEDDA. What has he told you—about this?

MRS. ELVSTED. He mentioned it, just once—quite vaguely.

HEDDA. So. And what did he say then?

MRS. ELVSTED. He said that when they broke up, she wanted to shoot him with a pistol.

HEDDA (*cold and composed*). Oh, come! One does not do that sort of thing here.

MRS. ELVSTED. No. And therefore I think she must have been that red-haired singer he once—

HEDDA. Yes, that may be so.

MRS. ELVSTED. Because I remember they used to say that she carried loaded weapons.

HEDDA. Oh—then obviously she must have been the one.

MRS. ELVSTED (*clutching her hands*). Yes, but just think, Hedda—now I hear that this singer—that she is in town again! Oh, I am so desperate—

HEDDA (*glancing towards the back parlor*). Ssh! Tesman is coming. (*Rising, whispers.*) Thea—all this must be kept a secret between you and me.

28 HENRIK IBSEN

MRS. ELVSTED (*springing up*). Oh, yes—yes! For heaven's sake—

JÖRGEN TESMAN, *with a letter in his hand, comes in from the right through the back parlor.*

TESMAN. So then—the letter is finished and ready.

HEDDA. That's good. And now Mrs. Elvsted wants to go too, I think. Wait a moment. I'll see you as far as the garden gate.

TESMAN. Hedda, perhaps Berte could take care of this?

HEDDA (*takes the letter*). I'll give her instructions.

BERTE *enters from the hall.*

BERTE. Mr. Brack is here and wants to extend greetings to the master and mistress.

HEDDA. Yes. Ask Mr. Brack to come in please. Also —look here—drop this letter in the mailbox.

BERTE (*taking the letter*). Yes, ma'am.

She opens the door for MR. BRACK *and goes out herself.* BRACK *is a man of 45—thickset, but well built and light in his movements. His face is roundish, with an aristocratic profile. His hair is short, still almost black, and carefully waved. His eyes are lively and sparkling. Thick eyebrows. His mustache is thick with clipped ends. His suit is well-cut, a little too youthful for him. He uses an eyeglass, which he now and then lets fall.*

MR. BRACK (*with his hat in his hand, bowing*). May one call so early in the day?

HEDDA. Yes, one may indeed.

TESMAN (*presses his hand*). You are welcome at any time. (*Making introductions.*) Mr. Brack—Miss Rysing—

HEDDA. Oh—!

BRACK (*bowing*). Ah—a particular pleasure——

HEDDA (*looks at him and laughs*). It's particularly interesting to have a look at you by daylight, Mr. Brack.

BRACK. Do you notice a difference?

HEDDA. Yes, a little younger, I think.

BRACK. Thanks from Yours Very Truly.

TESMAN. But what do you say about Hedda?— What? Doesn't she look flourishing? She has actually—

HEDDA. Oh, leave me out of it. Instead, thank Mr. Brack for all the trouble he has taken—

BRACK. Oh, come—it was a pleasure for me—

HEDDA. Yes, you are a good soul. But, my friend is standing here burning to go away. Excuse me, Mr. Brack. I'll be back almost at once.

Mutual good-byes. MRS. ELVSTED *and* HEDDA *go out by the hall door.*

BRACK. Well—is your wife fairly satisfied—?

TESMAN. Yes, we can't thank you enough. Of course, a little moving around here and there will be necessary, I gather. And we need one or two things. We shall have to buy a few odds and ends.

BRACK. Is that so? Really?

TESMAN. But you needn't bother yourself about them. Hedda said she would look after what we still need herself. —Why don't we sit down? Eh?

BRACK. Thanks, for just a moment. (*Sits beside the table.*) There is something I especially wanted to talk to you about, Tesman.

TESMAN. Indeed? Ah, I understand! (*Sitting down.*) I expect the serious part of the frolic is about to begin. Eh?

BRACK. Oh, the financial arrangements are not urgent yet. However, I could wish that we had gone about it a little more economically.

TESMAN. But that would never do, you know! Think of Hedda, my dear fellow! You, who know her so well —I couldn't possibly ask her to put up with an ordinary place.

BRACK. No, no—that is precisely the difficulty.

TESMAN. Also—fortunately—it can't be long before I get my appointment.

BRACK. Well, you know—such things often involve a long pull.

TESMAN. Have you heard something further? Eh?

BRACK. Not exactly something definite—(*interrupting himself*). But, I remember now—I can tell you one bit of news.

TESMAN. Well?

BRACK. Your old friend Ejlert Lövborg has come to town again.

TESMAN. I know that already.

BRACK. So? How did you hear of it?

TESMAN. She told me, the lady who went out with Hedda.

BRACK. Oh yes. What was her name? I didn't quite catch it.

TESMAN. Mrs. Elvsted.

BRACK. Aha—Sheriff Elvsted's wife. Yes—he's been staying up there in their part of the country.

TESMAN. And think, to my great delight, I hear that he is living a regular life again.

BRACK. Yes, so it is said.

TESMAN. Also, he's published a new book. What?

BRACK. Yes, he has.

TESMAN. And I hear it has made quite a sensation.

BRACK. It has made quite a remarkable sensation.

TESMAN. Just think—isn't that good to hear? He, with his extraordinary talents—I was so upset to think that he had gone to the bottom for good.

BRACK. That was what everybody thought about him.

TESMAN. But I don't understand what he will turn to now! What in the world will he make his living from? Eh?

During the last words, HEDDA *has entered by the hall door.*

HEDDA (*to* BRACK, *laughing, with a touch of scorn*). Tesman is always worrying about what people are going to live on.

TESMAN. Goodness—we were sitting talking about poor Ejlert Lövborg.

HEDDA (*glancing at him rapidly*). Oh, indeed? (*Sits in the arm chair beside the stove and asks indifferently*) What is the matter with *him?*

TESMAN. Well—he must have used up his inheritance long ago. And he can hardly write a new book every year. Right? Well—so I logically ask what is to become of him.

BRACK. Perhaps I can tell you something about that.

TESMAN. Indeed!

BRACK. You must remember that his relatives have a good deal of influence.

TESMAN. Oh, his relatives have completely washed their hands of him, unfortunately.

BRACK. They used to call him the hope of the family.

TESMAN. Used to, yes! But he completely put an end to that himself.

HEDDA. Who knows? (*Smiling slightly.*) Up at Sheriff Elvsted's I hear they have reformed him—

BRACK. And then this book that has come out—

TESMAN. Well, well, I hope to goodness they will help him one way or another. I have just written him. Hedda dear, I asked him to come and see us this evening.

BRACK. But my dear fellow you are coming to my stag dinner this evening. You promised on the pier last night.

HEDDA. Had you forgotten that, Tesman?

TESMAN. Yes, I had, completely.

BRACK. But you needn't be upset about it, because he won't come.

TESMAN. Why do you think that? Eh?

BRACK (*with a slight hesitation, rising and resting his hands on the back of his chair*). My dear Tesman— and you too Mrs. Tesman—I really must not keep you in ignorance about something that—that—

TESMAN. Something that concerns Ejlert—?

BRACK. Both you and him.

TESMAN. Well, my dear Brack, out with it.

BRACK. You must be prepared to find your appointment may not come quite as soon as you wished or expected.

TESMAN (*jumping up uneasily*). Has something gotten in the way? Eh?

BRACK. Possibly they may determine the appointment by competition—

TESMAN. Competition! Think of that, Hedda!

HEDDA (*leaning back farther in the chair*). Well, now!

TESMAN. But with whom? Surely not with—?

BRACK. Yes, exactly. With Ejlert Lövborg.

TESMAN (*clasping his hands*). No, no—that's absolutely unthinkable! Quite impossible! What?

BRACK. Mm—we may just possibly live to see it.

TESMAN. Well but, Brack—it would show the most incredible lack of consideration for me. (*Gesticulating.*) Yes, because—just think—I'm a married man! We married on these prospects, Hedda and I. Got ourselves in debt. And borrowed money from Aunt Julle, too.

Why, Good Heavens—I was as good as promised the position. Eh?

BRACK. Well, well, well—the post will probably go to you. But first there will be a competition.

HEDDA (*immovable*). Just think, Tesman—that will be almost like a duel.

TESMAN. Why, my dearest Hedda, how can you take it so lightly?

HEDDA (*as before*). I'm not in the least. I am really excited to see who will win.

BRACK. In any event, Mrs. Tesman, it is better to know how matters stand. I mean—before you start making the little purchases I hear you are threatening.

HEDDA. This won't make any difference.

BRACK. Indeed! Then there's no more to say. Good-bye! (*To* TESMAN.) When I take my afternoon stroll, I'll stop by and pick you up.

TESMAN. Oh yes, yes—I don't know whether I'm coming or going.

HEDDA (*reclining, holds out her hand*). Good-bye, Mr. Brack. And come again.

BRACK. Many thanks. Good-bye, good-bye.

TESMAN (*following him to the door*). Good-bye, my dear Brack! I hope you will excuse me—

BRACK *goes out by the hall door.*

TESMAN (*crosses the room*). Oh Hedda—one should never rush into an adventure. Eh?

HEDDA (*looks at him, smiling*). Did *you* do *that?*

TESMAN. Yes, dear—there's no denying it *was* adventurous to go and marry and set up housekeeping with nothing but expectations.

HEDDA. You may be right there.

TESMAN. Well—our charming house is ours anyways, Hedda! Imagine—the house we both dreamed of. Fell in love with, I might almost venture to say. Eh?

HEDDA (*rises slowly and wearily*). It was agreed that we would have a salon.

TESMAN. Yes, Good Lord—how that would have pleased me! Just think—to see you as hostess—in a highly—select circle! Eh? Well, well, well, for the present we shall have to make out by ourselves, Hedda. Except to entertain Aunt Julle now and then. —Oh, my dear, it should have been so very, very different—!

HEDDA. Of course I cannot have my servant in livery just yet.

TESMAN. Oh, no—unfortunately. A footman—that is quite out of the question, you know.

HEDDA. And the saddle-horse I was going to have—

TESMAN (*aghast*). The saddle-horse!

HEDDA. I suppose I must not even think of that now.

TESMAN. Good heavens, no! —That speaks for itself.

HEDDA (*goes up the room*). Well, I still have *one* thing to amuse myself with.

TESMAN (*beaming*). Oh, thank heaven for that! And what is that, Hedda? What?

HEDDA (*in the archway, looks at him with covert scorn*). My pistols, Jörgen.

TESMAN (*in alarm*). Your pistols!

HEDDA (*with cold eyes*). General Gabler's pistols.

She goes out through the inner room to the left.

TESMAN (*rushes up to the archway and calls after her*). No, for God's sake, dearest Hedda—don't touch those dangerous things! For my sake, Hedda! Eh?

Act Two

The room at the TESMANS' *as in the first act, except that the piano has been replaced by a secretary. Near the sofa on the left stands a smaller table. Most of the bouquets have been taken away.* MRS. ELVSTED'S *bouquet is on the larger table in front. It is afternoon.*

HEDDA, *in afternoon dress, is alone in the room. She stands by the open glass door, loading a revolver. The mate to it lies in an open pistol case on the secretary.*

HEDDA (*looks down into the garden*). Greetings again, Mr. Brack. How do you do?

BRACK (*calling from the stage, below*). Always the same, Mrs. Tesman!

HEDDA (*raising and aiming the pistol*). Now I shall shoot you, Mr. Brack!

BRACK (*still unseen*). No, no, no! Don't stand there aiming right at me!

HEDDA. That is what happens to people who always use back ways.

She fires.

BRACK (*nearer*). Have you gone mad—!
HEDDA. Goodness—did I hit you, possibly?
BRACK (*still outside*). Stop this foolishness!
HEDDA. Come in, then, Mr. Brack.

BRACK, *dressed for his stag party, enters through the glass door. He carries a light overcoat on his arm.*

BRACK. What the devil—do you still indulge in that sport? What are you shooting at?

HEDDA. Oh, I just stand here and shoot into the blue sky.

BRACK (*gently takes the pistol out of her hand*). With your permission, madam! (*Looks at it.*) Ah, this one—I know it very well. (*Looks around.*) Where is the case? Ah, here it is. (*Puts the pistol in the case and shuts it.*) Because we won't play that game any more today.

HEDDA. Well, what in heaven's name would you have me do with myself?

BRACK. Haven't you had any callers?

HEDDA (*at the secretary, putting the pistol-case in a drawer and shutting it*). No. As soon as he finished eating his lunch he ran off to his aunts. He didn't expect you so early.

BRACK. Mm—I didn't think of that. Stupid of me.

HEDDA (*turning her head to him*). Why stupid?

BRACK. Because if I had I should have come here a little—earlier.

HEDDA (*crossing the room*). Yes, and you wouldn't have found anyone at all. Because I have been in my room, changing.

BRACK. And isn't there a little chink in the door where one could negotiate?

HEDDA. You forgot to arrange for it.

BRACK. Again—stupid of me.

HEDDA. Well, we must just sit down here. And wait. Because Tesman is not likely to come back for a while.

BRACK. Indeed, indeed. Well, I shall have to be patient.

HEDDA *seats herself in the corner of the sofa.*
BRACK *lays his coat over the back of the nearest
chair and sits down, keeping his hat in his
hand. A short silence. They look at each other.*

HEDDA. Well?

BRACK (*in the same tone*). Well?

HEDDA. It was I who spoke first.

BRACK (*leaning a little forward*). Come, let us
have a cozy little gossip, Mrs.—Hedda.

HEDDA (*leaning further back in the sofa*). Doesn't
it seem like an age since we last talked? Of course
there were those few words last night and this
morning—but I hardly count those.

BRACK. You mean—just between ourselves? Tête-
à-tête, so to speak?

HEDDA. Well, yes. Something like that.

BRACK. I have passed here every single day and
wished that you were home again.

HEDDA. And all the time I have been wishing the
same thing.

BRACK. You? Really, Hedda? And I thought you
had been enjoying your trip so much.

HEDDA. Oh, yes, *you* can think it!

BRACK. But that is what Tesman always wrote in
his letters.

HEDDA. Oh, *him!* You see, he thinks there is
nothing so entertaining as to go and root around
in libraries. And to sit and make copies of old
parchments—or whatever they are.

BRACK (*with a hint of malice*). Well, that is his
vocation in life. At least in part.

HEDDA. Yes, of course. And no doubt when one
can—but *I!* Oh, no, my dear Mr. Brack—I have been
horribly bored.

BRACK (*sympathetically*). Do you really mean that?
In earnest?

HEDDA. Yes, just think of yourself in such a case—! To go for a whole half year without meeting a soul that knew of *our* circle. And with whom one could talk about the things that interest us.

BRACK. Yes, yes—that would also strike *me* as a loss.

HEDDA. And then, what was most intolerable of all—

BRACK. Well?

HEDDA. Always and forever to be together with— with one and the same person—

BRACK (*nodding agreement*). Early and late—yes. At all possible times.

HEDDA. I said "always and forever."

BRACK. Just so. But with our honest Tesman, I should have thought one would be able—

HEDDA. Tesman is—a scholar, my friend.

BRACK. No question.

HEDDA. And scholars are not exactly entertaining to travel with. Not for any length of time, at any rate.

BRACK. Not even—the scholar one *loves?*

HEDDA. Uh—don't use that sticky word!

BRACK (*taken aback*). What's that, Mrs. Hedda!

HEDDA (*half laughing, half irritated*). Yes, you should just try it, you should. To hear someone talk cultural history early and late—

BRACK. "Always and forever."

HEDDA. Yes, yes, yes! And all that about the domestic crafts of the middle ages—! That's the most revolting part of all.

BRACK (*looks searchingly at her*). But tell me—if that is true, how should I interpret your—? Mm—

HEDDA. That there should be a match between me and Jörgen Tesman, you mean?

BRACK. Well, yes, let's put it like that.

HEDDA. Good Lord, do you see that as anything so astonishing?

BRACK. I do and I don't—Hedda.

HEDDA. I had actually waltzed myself tired, my dear Mr. Brack. My day was done—(*with a slight shiver*). Oh, no—I will not say that. Nor think it either!

BRACK. I assure you you have no grounds for saying it.

HEDDA. Ah—grounds—(*watching him closely*). And Jörgen Tesman—after all, you must admit that he is a good man in every way.

BRACK. Good and dependable. No question.

HEDDA. And I can't find anything absolutely ridiculous about him—can you?

BRACK. Ridiculous? N—no—I wouldn't exactly say that—

HEDDA. So. And he is an indefatigable collector, at least. And it may very well be that he will get some place, in time.

BRACK (*hesitatingly*). I thought that you, like everybody else, expected he would become a distinguished man.

HEDDA (*with a gesture of fatigue*). Yes, so I did. And then, since he was so determined, with might and main, to support me—I really don't see why I shouldn't have accepted his offer.

BRACK. No, no. From *that* point of view—

HEDDA. It was more than my other admiring friends were willing to do for me, my dear Mr. Brack.

BRACK (*with a laugh*). Yes. I can hardly speak for the others. But as it concerns me, you know very well that I have always entertained a—a certain respect for the marriage tie. I mean in principle, Hedda.

HEDDA (*lightly*). Oh, I never had any hopes as far as *you* were concerned.

BRACK. All I ask is to have a small circle of close friends I can serve with a word and a deed and where I can feel free to come and go—as a trusted friend—

HEDDA. Of the man of the house, you mean?

BRACK (*bowing*). To be frank—first, of the lady. But next, of course, of the man, too. When you have—such a—may I call it, such a three-sided arrangement—it is a basis for great comfort to all concerned.

HEDDA. Yes, many times I longed for a third person on our journey. Uh—to be only a pair in a railroad compartment—!

BRACK. Fortunately now your wedding journey is over—

HEDDA (*shaking her head*). The journey has still a long way to go—a long way. I have only come to a station-stop.

BRACK. Well then, one gets off. And strolls around a little, Hedda.

HEDDA. I never get off.

BRACK. Is that so?

HEDDA. No—because there is always someone standing there, who—

BRACK (*with a laugh*). —who stares at your legs, you mean?

HEDDA. Precisely.

BRACK. Well, but, Good Lord—

HEDDA (*with a gesture of distaste*). I don't like that—I would rather stay seated—where I happen to be. In the compartment for two.

BRACK. Well, but suppose a third person were to climb in with the couple.

HEDDA. Ah—*that* is something else again!

BRACK. A trusted, understanding friend—

HEDDA. —entertaining on all sorts of lively subjects—

BRACK. —and without the least trace of the scholar!

HEDDA (*sighing audibly*). Yes, that is certainly a relief.

BRACK (*hears the front door opening and looks in that direction*). The triangle is completed.

HEDDA (*half aloud*). And so the train goes on.

JÖRGEN TESMAN *enters from the hall. He has a number of unbound books under his arm and in his pockets.*

TESMAN (*goes up to the table beside the corner sofa*). Whew, it was blessed hot today to lug these— all these books. (*Puts them on the table.*) I'm covered with perspiration, Hedda. Well, look here—are you here already, Brack? Eh? Berte didn't tell me.

BRACK (*rising*). I came up through the garden.

HEDDA. What are those books you brought?

TESMAN (*leafing through the books*). These are some new scholarly books that I had to have.

HEDDA. Scholarly books?

BRACK. Ah, yes, scholarly books, Mrs. Tesman.

BRACK *and* HEDDA *exchange a confidential smile.*

HEDDA. Do you really need more scholarly books?

TESMAN. Yes, Hedda dear, you can never have too many of them. Because you have to keep up with all that's written and printed.

HEDDA. Yes, of course, you must.

TESMAN (*searching among his books*). And see here —I've got hold of Ejlert Lövborg's new book too. (*Offering it to her.*) Would you like to look through it, Hedda? Eh?

HEDDA. No, thank you. Or rather—yes, perhaps later.

TESMAN. I leafed through it on the way.

BRACK. Well, what do you think of it—as a scholar?

TESMAN. I think it is remarkable how well-balanced

it is. He never used to write that way. (*Piling the books together.*) But now I'll take all these into my study. It will be delightful to cut the pages—! And also I must change my clothes. (*To* BRACK.) It isn't necessary for us to go right away? What?

BRACK. Oh goodness no—not for some time yet.

TESMAN. Well, then, I'll take my time. (*Starts to go with his books, but stops in the doorway, and turns.*) I just remembered, Hedda—Aunt Julle isn't coming to see you this evening.

HEDDA. She isn't? Is that business of the hat still bothering?

TESMAN. Far from it. How could you think such a thing of Aunt Julle? Just imagine—! But Aunt Rina is poorly, you see.

HEDDA. So she is all the time.

TESMAN. Yes, but today she is very much worse, poor dear.

HEDDA. Oh, then it's only natural for her sister to stay home with her. I must bear it as best I can.

TESMAN. But in spite of that, you can't think, dear, how delighted Aunt Julle seemed to be—because you had got so plump while we were traveling!

HEDDA (*half aside, rising*). Oh, those everlasting aunts!

TESMAN. What?

HEDDA (*going to the glass door*). Nothing.

TESMAN. Oh, all right.

He goes through the back parlor, out to the right.

BRACK. What was that hat you were talking about?

HEDDA. Oh, it was something to do with Miss Tesman this morning. She had put her hat down on that table. (*Looks at him and smiles.*) And I pretended I thought it was the maid's.

BRACK (*with a shake of the head*). But, my dear

Hedda, how could you do that! To that nice old lady!

HEDDA (*nervously crossing the room*). Well, you see—something just comes over me, just as that did. And when it does, I *can't* resist. (*Throws herself down in the armchair by the stove.*) Oh, I don't know how to explain it myself.

BRACK (*behind the armchair*). You aren't really happy—that's what's the matter.

HEDDA (*looking straight ahead*). I don't know why I should be—happy. Perhaps you can tell me why?

BRACK. Well—among other things, because you've got exactly the home you wanted to have.

HEDDA (*looks up at him and laughs*). Do you believe in that fairy-tale too?

BRACK. But isn't there something in it?

HEDDA. Oh, of course—there is *some*thing—

BRACK. Well?

HEDDA. There's *this* in it. I made use of Tesman to escort me home from evening parties, last summer—

BRACK. Unfortunately I had to go in quite a different direction—

HEDDA. That's true. You were going quite a different direction last summer.

BRACK (*laughing*). Shame on you, Hedda! Well, then—you and Tesman—?

HEDDA. Well, one evening we happened to come by here. And Tesman, poor fellow, was twisting and turning. Because he couldn't find a subject for light conversation. So I felt sorry for the scholar—

BRACK (*smiles doubtfully*). *You* did? Mm—

HEDDA. Yes, I actually did. And so—to help him out of his distress—I happened, quite without thinking, to say that I would like to live in this villa.

BRACK. No more than that?

HEDDA. Not *that* evening.

BRACK. But afterwards?

HEDDA. Yes, my thoughtlessness had consequences, Mr. Brack.

BRACK. Unfortunately, Hedda, thoughtlessness does, more often than not.

HEDDA. Thanks! So, in this enthusiasm for the villa of Secretary Falk's widow, Jörgen Tesman and I came to an understanding, you see. *That* brought after it the engagement, and the marriage, and the wedding journey, and everything else. Yes, yes, Mr. Brack, I almost said, one must lie in the bed one has made.

BRACK. This is delicious! And as a matter of fact you didn't give a damn about it.

HEDDA. No, God knows, I didn't.

BRACK. Yes, but now? Now that we've made it at least a little cozy for you?

HEDDA. Uh—I seem to smell lavender and attar of roses in every room. —But perhaps the odor came with Aunt Julle.

BRACK (*laughing*). No, I think it was left behind by the late Mrs. Falk.

HEDDA. Yes, there is a smell of death about it. It reminds me of a bouquet—the day after the ball. (*Clasps her hands behind her head, leans back in her chair and looks at him.*) Oh, my dear Mr. Brack— you can't imagine how horribly bored I shall be out here.

BRACK. Shouldn't life have some interest or other for you as well, Hedda?

HEDDA. An interest that might have a temptation in it?

BRACK. If possible, of course.

HEDDA. Heaven knows what kind of interest that could be. Many times I have thought of—(*She breaks off.*) But that would never do either.

BRACK. Who knows? Let me hear what it is.

HEDDA. Whether I could get Tesman to go into politics, I mean.

BRACK (*laughing*). Tesman? No, you must realize that—anything like politics is not in his world—not for him at all.

HEDDA. No, I realize that—but suppose I could get him into it just the same?

BRACK. Yes—what gratification would there be for you in that? When he is not fitted for it. Why should you want to drive him into it?

HEDDA. Because I am bored, do you hear! (*A pause.*) So you think it will be quite out of the question for Tesman to become a member of the cabinet?

BRACK. Mm—you see, Hedda—to do that he would have to be a fairly rich man.

HEDDA (*rising impatiently*). Yes, there you have it! It's this respectable poverty I've got myself into—! (*Crosses the room.*) That's what makes life so wretched! So completely ludicrous! —For that's just what it is, ludicrous!

BRACK. Now, I think the blame lies somewhere else.

HEDDA. Where, then?

BRACK. You have never gone through anything that really stimulated you.

HEDDA. Anything serious, you mean?

BRACK. Yes, you can call it that. But now—perhaps, it is coming——?

HEDDA (*with a toss of her head*). Oh, you're thinking about the fuss over that wretched professorship! But that is Tesman's business. I refuse to waste a thought on it.

BRACK. No, no, skip all that. But now suppose that there comes—what people—in rather elegant language —call a serious, demanding responsibility on you?

(*Smiling.*) A new responsibility, my dear Hedda?

HEDDA (*angrily*). Be quiet! You will never live to see anything like that!

BRACK (*warily*). We will talk about this again in a year's time—at the very most.

HEDDA (*curtly*). I have no leaning towards such things, Mr. Brack. Not for responsibilities.

BRACK. Shouldn't you, like most other women, have a natural aptitude for a vocation that—?

HEDDA (*at the glass door*). Oh, be quiet, I tell you! Often I have thought that I have an aptitude for just one thing in the world.

BRACK (*near her*). And what is that, if I may ask?

HEDDA (*looking out*). To bore the life out of myself. Now you know it. (*Turns, looks towards the back room and laughs.*) Yes, as I thought! Here's our Professor.

BRACK (*warning*). Come, come, come, Hedda!

JÖRGEN TESMAN, *dressed for the party, with his gloves and hat in his hand, enters from the right through the back parlor.*

TESMAN. Hedda—isn't there any message from Ejlert Lövborg? Eh?

HEDDA. No.

TESMAN. So, then! You'll see, we will have him here shortly.

BRACK. Do you really think he will come?

TESMAN. Yes, I am almost sure of it. For that must have been a mere floating rumor—what you told us this morning.

BRACK. So?

TESMAN. Yes. At least Aunt Julle said she didn't think for worlds that he would ever stand in my way again. Think of that!

BRACK. Well, then, everything is satisfactory.

TESMAN (*folding his gloves in his hat, and placing it on a chair at the right*). Yes, but I really ought to wait for him until the last minute.

BRACK. We have plenty of time for that. No one will show up at my house before seven—or seven-thirty.

TESMAN. Well then, we can keep Hedda company till then. And see what happens? Eh?

HEDDA (*putting Brack's hat and overcoat on the corner sofa*). And if worst comes to worst, Mr. Lövborg can stay here with me.

BRACK (*offering to take his things*). Oh, allow me, Mrs. Tesman! —What do you mean by "the worst"?

HEDDA. In case he won't go with you and Tesman.

TESMAN (*looks doubtfully at her*). But Hedda, dear —do you think it would be quite proper for him to stay here with you? Eh? Remember, Aunt Julle can't come.

HEDDA. No, but Mrs. Elvsted is coming. And the three of us can drink a cup of tea together.

TESMAN. Oh, yes, *that* will be all right.

BRACK (*with a smile*). And perhaps that will be safest for him, too.

HEDDA. Why so?

BRACK. Good Lord, Mrs. Tesman, you always used to gibe at my little stag parties. You said, they were only fit for men of the most rigid principles.

HEDDA. But no doubt Mr. Lövborg's principles are strict enough now. A reformed sinner—

BERTE *appears at the hall door.*

BERTE. Ma'am, there's a gentleman would like to see you—

HEDDA. Yes, let him come in.

TESMAN (*softly*). I'm sure it is he! Just imagine!

EJLERT LÖVBORG *enters from the hall. He is slight and lean, and about* TESMAN's *age. However, he looks older and somewhat worn out. His hair and beard are dark brown, his face long and pale, but with two patches of color on the cheekbones. He is well dressed in a new black suit with dark gloves and a top hat. He stops near the door and makes a rapid bow. He seems somewhat embarrassed.*

TESMAN (*goes up to him and shakes him warmly by the hand*). Well, my dear Ejlert—so at last we meet again!

LÖVBORG (*in a subdued voice*). Thanks for your letter, Jörgen. (*Approaching* HEDDA.) May I offer my hand to you also, Mrs. Tesman?

HEDDA (*taking his hand*). Welcome, Mr. Lövborg. (*With a gesture.*) I don't know whether you two gentlemen—?

LÖVBORG (*bowing slightly*). Mr. Brack, I think.

BRACK (*doing likewise*). Oh, yes. Because, some years ago—

TESMAN (*to Lövborg, putting his hands on his shoulders*). And now you must behave as if you were in your own home, Ejlert! Mustn't he, Hedda? For you're going to settle down in the city, I hear? Eh?

LÖVBORG. I intend to.

TESMAN. Now that is quite reasonable. Listen, Ejlert—I have just got hold of your new book. But I really haven't had time to read it yet.

LÖVBORG. You can spare yourself the trouble.

TESMAN. What do you mean?

LÖVBORG. Because there is nothing much in it.

TESMAN. Just think—that you should say such a thing!

BRACK. But it has been very much praised, I hear.

LÖVBORG. Exactly what I was after. So I wrote a book that everyone would agree with.

BRACK. Very judicious.

TESMAN. But my dear Ejlert—!

LÖVBORG. Because I want to try to build myself up to a place in the world again. To begin over.

TESMAN (*a little embarrassed*). Yes, you really want to do that? What?

LÖVBORG (*smiling, puts down his hat and draws a packet, wrapped in paper, from his coat pocket*). But when this one comes out—Jörgen Tesman—this one you must read. For *this* is the first real book. The one I have put myself into.

TESMAN. Indeed? And what is it exactly?

LÖVBORG. It is the sequel.

TESMAN. The sequel to what?

LÖVBORG. To the book.

TESMAN. To the new book?

LÖVBORG. That's it.

TESMAN. Why, my dear Ejlert—the new book comes right up to our own time.

LÖVBORG. Yes it does. And this one deals with the future.

TESMAN. With the future! But, good heavens, we don't know anything about that!

LÖVBORG. No. But there is a thing or two to say about it, just the same. (*Opens the packet.*) Here you see—

TESMAN. Why, that's not your handwriting.

LÖVBORG. I dictated it. (*Leafing through it.*) It's divided into two parts. The first deals with the forces that will determine the civilization of the future. And this is the second—(*running through the pages at the end*)—which concerns the nature of civilization in the future.

TESMAN. Amazing! It would never occur to me to write about anything like that.

HEDDA (*at the glass door, tapping on the pane*). Mm—no, indeed.

LÖVBORG (*replacing the manuscript in its paper and putting the packet on the table*). I brought it with me because I thought I might read a little of it to you this evening.

TESMAN. That was very good of you, Ejlert. But this evening—? (*Glancing at* BRACK.) I don't quite see how it can be arranged—

LÖVBORG. Well, then, another time. There's no hurry.

BRACK. I should tell you, Mr. Lövborg—there is a little gathering at my house this evening. Mainly for Tesman, you know—

LÖVBORG (*looking for his hat*). Oh—then I won't detain you—

BRACK. No, but listen. Won't you give me the pleasure of coming with us?

LÖVBORG (*shortly and firmly*). No, I can't. But thanks, anyway.

BRACK. Oh, come. You must. We shall be a small select circle. And I promise you we shall be quite "lively" as Hed—as Mrs. Tesman says.

LÖVBORG. That I don't doubt. But nevertheless—

BRACK. So you could bring your manuscript with you and read it to Tesman at my house. I have plenty of room.

TESMAN. Yes, think of that, Ejlert—you could do that! Eh?

HEDDA (*interposing*). But, dear, if Mr. Lövborg really doesn't want to! I am sure Mr. Lövborg would much rather stay here and have supper with me.

LÖVBORG (*looking at her*). With you, Mrs. Tesman?

HEDDA. And with Mrs. Elvsted, too.

LÖVBORG. Ah— (*Lightly.*) I met her for a moment this morning—

HEDDA. Did you? Well, she is coming out here. So you *must* stay, Mr. Lövborg. Otherwise she will have no one to escort her home.

LÖVBORG. That's true. Many thanks, Mrs. Tesman—then I'll stay.

HEDDA. I will just give the maid one or two orders—

She goes to the hall door and rings. BERTE *enters.* HEDDA *talks to her in a whisper and points towards the back parlor.* BERTE *nods and goes out again.*

TESMAN (*at the same time, to Lövborg*). Listen, Ejlert—is this new topic—the future—the one that you are going to lecture on?

LÖVBORG. Yes.

TESMAN. Because I heard at the bookstore you are going to deliver a series of lectures this fall.

LÖVBORG. I intend to. You must not blame me for this, Tesman.

TESMAN. Oh, my goodness, no! But—!

LÖVBORG. I can understand how it may go against the grain with you.

TESMAN (*cast down*). Ah, just for my sake I can hardly expect you to—

LÖVBORG. But I'm going to wait till you have been appointed.

TESMAN. You are going to wait! Yes, but—yes, but—aren't you in the competition? What?

LÖVBORG. No, I only want to win over you in men's minds.

TESMAN. Why, Good Lord—then Aunt Julle was right after all! Oh yes—that was the way it was, I knew it! Hedda! Just think, dear—Ejlert Lövborg isn't going to stand in our way after all!

HEDDA (*curtly*). Our way? Leave me out of it.

She goes up toward the back parlor where BERTE *is arranging a tray with decanters and glasses on the table.* HEDDA *nods her approval and comes forward again.* BERTE *goes out.*

TESMAN (*at the same time*). And you, Mr. Brack— what do you say about this? What?

BRACK. Well, I say that honor and victory—mm— these can indeed be very pleasant—

TESMAN. Yes, they certainly can. But all the same—

HEDDA (*looking at Tesman with a hard smile*). You look as if you'd been struck by lightning.

TESMAN. Yes—close to it—I feel almost—

BRACK. It was indeed a thunderstorm that just passed over us, Mrs. Tesman—

HEDDA (*pointing towards the back parlor*). Will you gentlemen come and have a glass of cold punch?

BRACK (*looking at his watch*). A stirrup cup? Yes, that would be just right.

TESMAN. An excellent idea, Hedda! Just the thing! I am in such a good mood now that I have learned—

HEDDA. You too Mr. Lövborg?

LÖVBORG (*with a gesture of refusal*). No, thanks very much. Nothing for me.

BRACK. Why, Good Lord—cold punch is not poison, to my knowledge.

LÖVBORG. Not for everyone, perhaps.

HEDDA. I will keep Mr. Lövborg company in the meantime.

TESMAN. Yes, yes, Hedda, dear. You do that.

He and BRACK *go into the back parlor, seat themselves, drink punch, smoke cigarettes and carry on a lively conversation during the following scene.* EJLERT LÖVBORG *remains standing beside the stove.* HEDDA *goes to the secretary.*

HEDDA (*raising her voice a little*). Now I'll show you some photographs if you'd be interested. Tesman and I—we made a trip through the Tyrol on our way home.

She takes up an album, and places it on the table beside the sofa, in the further corner of which she sits down. EJLERT LÖVBORG *approaches, stops, and looks at her. Then he takes a chair and sits down at her left, with his back toward the back parlor.*

HEDDA (*opening the album*). Do you see this range of mountains, Mr. Lövborg? It's the Ortler Group. Tesman has written it underneath. Here it is: "The Ortler Group near Meran."

LÖVBORG (*who has been staring at her, says softly and slowly*). Hedda—Gabler!

HEDDA (*glancing hastily at him*). Now! Hush!

LÖVBORG (*repeats softly*). Hedda Gabler!

HEDDA (*looking at the album*). That was my name in the old days. The days—when we two knew each other.

LÖVBORG. And hereafter—and for the rest of my life—I must break myself of saying Gabler.

HEDDA (*still turning over the pages*). Yes, you must. And I think you ought to practice at once. The sooner the better, I think.

LÖVBORG (*with indignation*). Hedda Gabler married? And married to—Jörgen Tesman!

HEDDA. Yes—so it turned out.

LÖVBORG. Oh, Hedda, Hedda—my dear, how could you throw yourself away like that!

HEDDA (*looks quickly at him*). Now, none of that here! I can't allow this!

LÖVBORG. What do you mean?

TESMAN *comes into the room and crosses to the sofa.*

HEDDA (*hears him coming and says in an indifferent tone*). And this, Mr. Lövborg, is a view from the Val d'Ampezzo. Just look at these peaks! (*Looks up at* TESMAN *affectionately.*) What is it these curious peaks are called, dear?

TESMAN. Let's see. Oh, those are the Dolomites.

HEDDA. Ah, yes! —Those are the Dolomites, Mr. Lövborg.

TESMAN. Hedda, dear—I just wanted to ask whether we shouldn't bring you a little punch after all? For you, at least.——What?

HEDDA. Yes, do, please. And perhaps a few cakes.

TESMAN. No cigarettes?

HEDDA. No.

TESMAN. Right.

He goes into the back parlor and out to the right. BRACK *remains seated and from time to time glances at* HEDDA *and* LÖVBORG.

LÖVBORG (*softly, as before*). Answer me now, Hedda dear—how could you go and do such a thing?

HEDDA (*apparently absorbed in the album*). If you persist in calling me "dear" I won't talk to you.

LÖVBORG. May I not say "dear" even when we are alone?

HEDDA. No. You may have the right to think it. But you mustn't say it.

LÖVBORG. Ah, I understand. It is an offense against your love—for Jörgen Tesman.

HEDDA (*glances at him and smiles*). Love? No, now that's good!

LÖVBORG. So it's not love!

HEDDA. But no infidelity of any sort. That I won't stand for.

LÖVBORG. Hedda—answer me just one thing—
HEDDA. Hush!

TESMAN *enters with a small tray from the back parlor.*

TESMAN. There you are! Here come the good things.

He puts the tray on the table.

HEDDA. Why did you fetch it and serve it yourself?
TESMAN (*filling the glasses*). Why, because I think it's such a pleasure to wait on you, Hedda.
HEDDA. Now you have filled both glasses. And Mr. Lövborg doesn't want any—
TESMAN. No, but Mrs. Elvsted will be here soon.
HEDDA. Yes, that's so—Mrs. Elvsted—
TESMAN. Did you forget about her? What?
HEDDA. We sat here so completely absorbed in these. (*Shows him a picture.*) Do you remember this little village?
TESMAN. Oh, it's the one just below the Brenner Pass. It was *there* we stayed over night—
HEDDA. —and met all those lively tourists.
TESMAN. Yes, that was the place. Think—if we could only have had *you* with us, Ejlert! Ah!

He returns to the back parlor and sits beside BRACK.

LÖVBORG. Answer me just this one thing, Hedda—
HEDDA. Well?
LÖVBORG. Was there no love in your friendship for me either? Not a flicker—not a gleam of love in it?
HEDDA. Yes, I wonder if there was? To me it seems as though we were two good comrades. Two really intimate friends. (*Smilingly.*) *You* especially were completely candid.
LÖVBORG. It was you who wanted me to be that way.

HEDDA. As I look back on all that, there seems to be something beautiful, something fascinating—something that seems to me almost courageous—in that secret relationship—that comradeship, that no living person had any inkling of.

LÖVBORG. Yes, isn't that so, Hedda! Wasn't there?—When I came up to your father's in the afternoon—And the General sat over by the window reading his papers—with his back turned—

HEDDA. And we two on the corner sofa—

LÖVBORG. Always with the same magazine in front of us—

HEDDA. For want of a photograph album, yes.

LÖVBORG. Yes, Hedda—and when I confessed to you—! Told you things about myself that nobody else knew in those days! Told you how I had wandered about whole days and nights. Stayed drunk day after day. Ah, Hedda—what sort of power did you have that forced me to confess these things?

HEDDA. Do you think it was some power in me?

LÖVBORG. Yes, how else can I explain it to myself? And all those—those indirect questions you used to put to me—

HEDDA. And which you understood perfectly well—

LÖVBORG. To think that you could sit and question me like that! Quite boldly!

HEDDA. With indirect questions, remember.

LÖVBORG. Yes, but boldly too. Cross-question me about—about everything like that!

HEDDA. And to think that you could answer, Mr. Lövborg.

LÖVBORG. Yes, that's just what I can't understand—as I look back on it. But tell me this, Hedda—wasn't it love at the bottom of our friendship? Wasn't it as if you wanted to wash me clean—if I came to you and confessed? Wasn't it so?

HEDDA. No, not quite.

LÖVBORG. What was your motive, then?

HEDDA. Do you find it incomprehensible that a young girl—when it can be done—in secret—

LÖVBORG. Well?

HEDDA. —That she would like to have a little peep into a world that——

LÖVBORG. That—?

HEDDA. —that she is supposed to know nothing about?

LÖVBORG. So that was all it was?

HEDDA. That too. That too,—I think *nearly* all.

LÖVBORG. Comradeship in the quest for experience. But why couldn't *that* at least, have gone on?

HEDDA. You yourself were to blame.

LÖVBORG. You were the one who broke it off.

HEDDA. Yes, that was when I saw the danger of something serious entering into our comradeship. Shame on you, Ejlert Lövborg, how could you bring yourself to lay hands on—on your innocent comrade?

LÖVBORG (*clenching his hands*). Oh, why didn't you finish it! Why didn't you shoot me down, when you threatened to!

HEDDA. That shows you how frightened I am of scandal.

LÖVBORG. Yes, Hedda, you are a coward underneath.

HEDDA. A terrible coward. (*Changing her tone.*) But it was lucky for you. And now you have consoled yourself most satisfactorily up at the Elvsteds'.

LÖVBORG. I know what Thea has told you.

HEDDA. And you perhaps have told her something about us two?

LÖVBORG. Not a word. She is too stupid to understand such things.

HEDDA. Stupid?

LÖVBORG. About such things she's stupid.

HEDDA. And I'm a coward. (*Bends over towards him, without looking him in the face, and says more softly:*) But now *I* will tell *you* something.

LÖVBORG (*eagerly*). Well?

HEDDA. *That,* my not daring to shoot you down—

LÖVBORG. Yes?!

HEDDA. ——*that* was not my worst cowardice—that evening.

LÖVBORG (*looks at her a moment, understands and whispers passionately*). Oh, Hedda! Hedda Gabler! Now I begin to see a hidden ground beneath our comradeship! You, dear, and I! After all then, it was your passion for experience—

HEDDA (*softly, with a sharp glance*). Watch out! Don't jump to conclusions!

Twilight has begun to fall. The hall door is opened from without by BERTE.

HEDDA (*closes the album with a snap and calls smilingly*). Ah, at last! My darling Thea—come right in!

MRS. ELVSTED *enters from the hall. She is in evening dress. The door is closed behind her.*

HEDDA (*still seated, stretches out her arms towards her*). Thea, my sweet—you can't imagine how I have been longing for you!

MRS. ELVSTED, *in passing, exchanges slight salutations with the gentlemen in the back parlor, then goes up to the table and gives* HEDDA *her hand.* EJLERT LÖVBORG *has risen. He and* MRS. ELVSTED *greet each other silently with a nod.*

MRS. ELVSTED. Perhaps I should go in and talk with your husband for a moment?

HEDDA. Oh, not at all. Let them be. They will be going soon.

MRS. ELVSTED. Are they going out?

HEDDA. Yes, they are going to a stag party.

MRS. ELVSTED. (*To* LÖVBORG.) Not *you*, though?

LÖVBORG. No.

HEDDA. Mr. Lövborg—he's staying with us here.

MRS. ELVSTED (*takes a chair and is about to sit by his side*). Oh, how nice it is to be here!

HEDDA. No thank you, my little Thea. Not *there!* You come right over here beside me. I will sit in between you.

MRS. ELVSTED. Just as you like.

She goes round the table and sits on the sofa at HEDDA's *right.* LÖVBORG *sits down again in his chair.*

LÖVBORG (*after a short pause, to* HEDDA). Isn't she lovely to look at?

HEDDA (*lightly stroking* MRS. ELVSTED's *hair*). Just to look at?

LÖVBORG. Yes. For *we* two—she and I—we really are two comrades. We have absolute faith in each other. And so we can sit and talk with perfect frankness—

HEDDA. Not indirectly, Mr. Lövborg?

LÖVBORG. Well—

MRS. ELVSTED (*clinging close to* HEDDA). Oh how fortunate I am, Hedda. For—imagine—he says I've been an inspiration to him, too.

HEDDA (*looks at her with a smile*). No, does he say that, dear?

LÖVBORG. And she has such courage to act, Mrs. Tesman!

MRS. ELVSTED. My goodness—*me,* courage!

LÖVBORG. Enormous—when it concerns a comrade.

HEDDA. *Courage!* Oh, if one only had *that.*

LÖVBORG. What do you mean?

HEDDA. Then perhaps one might at least be able to live life. (*With a sudden change of tone.*) But now, my dearest Thea—you must drink a nice glass of cold punch.

MRS. ELVSTED. No thanks—I never drink anything like that.

HEDDA. Well then, *you,* Mr. Lövborg.

LÖVBORG. Thank you, I don't either!

HEDDA (*looks fixedly at him*). Even if I want you to?

LÖVBORG. Makes no difference.

HEDDA (*laughing*). Then, poor thing that I am, I have no sort of power over you.

LÖVBORG. Not where *that's* concerned.

HEDDA. Joking aside, I really think you ought to. For your own good.

MRS. ELVSTED. Oh, but Hedda—!

LÖVBORG. Why so?

HEDDA. Or rather on account of other people.

LÖVBORG. Indeed?

HEDDA. Otherwise people might come to think that you—deep down inside—that you did not feel secure —quite sure of yourself.

MRS. ELVSTED (*softly*). Oh no, Hedda—

LÖVBORG. People can think what they like—for the present.

MRS. ELVSTED (*joyfully*). Yes, exactly!

HEDDA. I saw it so plainly with Mr. Brack just now.

LÖVBORG. What did you see?

HEDDA. He smiled so scornfully when you didn't dare to go with them to the table in there.

LÖVBORG. Didn't dare! I naturally wanted to stay here and talk with you.

MRS. ELVSTED. That's only reasonable, Hedda!

HEDDA. But Mr. Brack couldn't guess that. But I also saw him smile and glance at Tesman when you didn't dare go with them to this silly little stag party either.

LÖVBORG. Dare! Did you say I didn't dare?

HEDDA. I didn't. But that's how Mr. Brack took it.

LÖVBORG. Well, let him.

HEDDA. Then you're not going with them?

LÖVBORG. I remain here with you and Thea.

MRS. ELVSTED. Yes, Hedda—you can believe that!

HEDDA (*smiling and nodding approval at* LÖVBORG). How firm a foundation! Firm principles forever! There, that's what a man should be! (*Turns to* MRS. ELVSTED *and pats her.*) Now, wasn't that what I said, when you came in here this morning in such a state of distraction—

LÖVBORG (*surprised*). Distraction!

MRS. ELVSTED (*terrified*). Hedda— Oh Hedda!—

HEDDA. See for yourself! There wasn't the slightest need for you to come here in such deadly anxiety— (*Interrupting herself.*) There! Now the three of us can be cheerful!

LÖVBORG (*who has given a start*). Ah—what is all this about, Mrs. Tesman?

MRS. ELVSTED. Oh, my God, my God, Hedda! What are you saying! What are you doing!

HEDDA. Do be calm! That disgusting Mr. Brack is sitting there keeping his eye on you.

LÖVBORG. *Worried* to death. About me.

MRS. ELVSTED (*softly and piteously*). Oh, Hedda— now you've upset everything for me.

LÖVBORG (*looks fixedly at her for a moment. His face is distorted.*) So *that* was my comrade's complete faith in me?

MRS. ELVSTED (*imploringly*). Oh, my dearest friend —first you must hear!

LÖVBORG (*takes one of the glasses of punch, raises it to his lips and says in a low husky voice*). Your health, Thea!

He empties the glass, puts it down, and takes a second.

MRS. ELVSTED (*softly*). Oh Hedda, Hedda—how could you want this to happen?

HEDDA. Want it? Me? Are you crazy?

LÖVBORG. And to your health, too, Mrs. Tesman. Thanks for the truth. Long live the truth!

He empties the glass and is about to refill it.

HEDDA (*lays her hands on his arm*). Come, come— no more for the present. Remember you are going to a party.

MRS. ELVSTED. No, no, no!

HEDDA. Hush! They are sitting there looking at you.

LÖVBORG (*putting down the glass*). Now, Thea— tell the truth—

MRS. ELVSTED. Yes!

LÖVBORG. Did the Sheriff know that you had come here after me?

MRS. ELVSTED (*wringing her hands*). Oh, Hedda— you hear what he's asking about?

LÖVBORG. Was there an agreement between you and him that you should come to the city and watch out for me? Perhaps it was the Sheriff himself who made you do it? Aha, my dear—no doubt he needed me in his office again? Or does he miss me at the card table?

MRS. ELVSTED (*softly, in agony*). Oh, Lövborg, Lövborg—!

LÖVBORG (*on the point of filling another glass*). A health to the old Sheriff too!

HEDDA (*stopping him*). No more just now. Remember you are going to read your manuscript to Tesman.

LÖVBORG (*calmly, putting down the glass*). It was stupid, Thea, all this—to take it this way, I mean. Don't be angry with me, my dear, dear comrade. You shall see—you and the others—that if I was fallen once. —Now I have raised myself again! With *your* help, Thea.

MRS. ELVSTED (*radiant with joy*). Oh, God be praised—!

BRACK *in the meantime has looked at his watch. He and* TESMAN *get up and come into the front room.*

BRACK (*takes his coat and hat*). Well, Mrs. Tesman, our time is up.

HEDDA. I suppose it is.

LÖVBORG (*rising*). Mine too, Mr. Brack.

MRS. ELVSTED (*softly and imploringly*). Oh, Lövborg—don't do it!

HEDDA (*pinching her arm*). They'll hear you!

MRS. ELVSTED (*gives a suppressed cry*)!

LÖVBORG (*to* BRACK). You were so kind as to invite me to join you.

BRACK. Oh, are you coming after all?

LÖVBORG. Yes, many thanks.

BRACK. I'm delighted—

LÖVBORG (*to* TESMAN, *putting the parcel of manuscript in his pocket*). Because I'd like to show you one or two bits before I send it off.

TESMAN. Now just think—that will be nice! But, Hedda dear, how will you get Mrs. Elvsted home? What?

HEDDA. Oh, that can be managed somehow.

LÖVBORG (*looking towards the ladies*). Mrs. Elvsted? Of course, I'll come back and fetch her. (*Approaching.*) Around ten o'clock, Mrs. Tesman? Will that do?

HEDDA. Certainly. That will do nicely.

TESMAN. Well, then, that's all settled. But you mustn't expect me quite so early, Hedda.

HEDDA. My dear, you may stay as long—as long as you want to.

MRS. ELVSTED (*trying to conceal her anxiety*). Mr. Lövborg—then I'm to wait here till you come.

LÖVBORG (*with his hat in his hand*). If you please, Mrs. Elvsted.

BRACK. All aboard for the excursion train, gentlemen! I trust we shall have a lively time, as a certain fair lady puts it.

HEDDA. Ah, if only the fair lady could be present unseen—!

BRACK. Why unseen?

HEDDA. So she could hear a little of your liveliness uncensored, Mr. Brack.

BRACK (*laughing*). I should not recommend it to the fair lady.

TESMAN (*also laughing*). You certainly take the prize, Hedda! Think of that!

BRACK. Well, good-bye, good-bye, ladies!

LÖVBORG (*bowing*). About ten o'clock, then.

BRACK, LÖVBORG *and* TESMAN *go out by the hall door. At the same time,* BERTE *enters from the back parlor with a lighted lamp, which she places on the living room table; she goes out by the way she came in.*

MRS. ELVSTED (*who has risen and is wandering restlessly about the room*). Hedda—Hedda—what is going to happen?

HEDDA. At ten o'clock—he will come. I can see him before my eyes. With vine leaves in his hair. Flushed and fearless—

MRS. ELVSTED. Oh, I hope it will turn out so well.

HEDDA. And then, you see—then he will have influence over himself again. Then he will be a free man for the rest of his days.

MRS. ELVSTED. Oh, God, yes—if only he will come as you see him now!

HEDDA. So and no other way will he come! (*Rises and approaches Thea.*) Have doubts about him as much as you like. I believe in him. And now we shall see. . . .

MRS. ELVSTED. There is something behind your actions, Hedda!

HEDDA. Yes, there is. For once in my life I want to influence a human fate.

MRS. ELVSTED. Haven't you done that?

HEDDA. No—not ever.

MRS. ELVSTED. Not your husband's?

HEDDA. Now, that would really be worth the trouble. Oh, if you could only understand how poor I am! And you have the chance to be so rich. (*Clasps her passionately in her arms.*) I think I'll burn your hair off after all.

MRS. ELVSTED. Let me go! Let me go! I am afraid of you, Hedda!

BERTE (*in the archway*). Tea is ready in the dining room, ma'am.

HEDDA. Good. We're coming.

MRS. ELVSTED. No, no, no! I would rather go home alone! Right now!

HEDDA. Nonsense. First you must have a cup of tea, silly. And then—at ten o'clock—Ejlert Lövborg will come—with vine leaves in his hair.

She drags MRS. ELVSTED *almost by main force towards the archway.*

Act Three

The room at the TESMANS'. *The curtains over the
middle archway and the glass door are drawn together. The lamp, half turned down, shaded, is burning on the table. In the stove, the door of which
stands open, there has been a fire, now nearly burned
out.*

MRS. ELVSTED, *wrapped in a large shawl, sits close
to the stove, sunk back in the armchair, with her feet
on a footstool.* HEDDA, *fully dressed, is sleeping on the
sofa, with a blanket over her.*

MRS. ELVSTED (*after a pause, suddenly sits up in
her chair and listens eagerly. Then she sinks back again
wearily, crying softly*). Not yet!— Oh God— Oh God
—not yet!

BERTE *slips cautiously in by the hall door. She is
carrying a letter.*

MRS. ELVSTED (*turns and whispers eagerly*). Well—
has anyone come?

BERTE (*softly*). Yes, a girl came with this letter
just now.

MRS. ELVSTED (*quickly, holding out her hand*). A
letter! Give it to me!

BERTE. No, it's for the doctor, ma'am.

MRS. ELVSTED. Ah, so.

BERTE. It was Miss Tesman's maid came with it. I'll
put it here on the table.

MRS. ELVSTED. Yes, do that.

BERTE (*putting down the letter*). I think I better put out the lamp. It's smoking.

MRS. ELVSTED. Yes, put it out. It'll be light now very soon.

BERTE (*putting out the lamp*). It *is* light already, ma'am.

MRS. ELVSTED. Yes, broad daylight! And not come home yet—!

BERTE. Lord bless you, ma'am—I thought it would be like this.

MRS. ELVSTED. You thought so?

BERTE. Yes. When I saw that a certain person had come to the city again, well—and went off with them. For we've heard a good deal about that gentleman before this.

MRS. ELVSTED. Don't speak so loud. You'll wake Mrs. Tesman.

BERTE (*looks towards the sofa and sighs*). No, my sakes—let her sleep, poor thing. —Should I put a little more in the stove?

MRS. ELVSTED. Thanks, not for me.

BERTE. Oh, very good.

She goes out quickly by the hall door.

HEDDA (*awakened by the shutting of the door, looks up*). What's that—?

MRS. ELVSTED. It was only the maid—

HEDDA (*glancing about her*). Oh, here—! Yes, I remember now. —(*Sits erect upon the sofa, stretching and rubbing her eyes.*) What time is it, Thea?

MRS. ELVSTED (*looking at her watch*). It's after seven.

HEDDA. What time did Tesman come home?

MRS. ELVSTED. He hasn't come.

HEDDA. Not come home yet?

MRS. ELVSTED (*rising*). No one has come.

HEDDA. And we sat here and kept awake and waited like this till four o'clock—

MRS. ELVSTED (*wringing her hands*). And how I waited for him!

HEDDA (*yawns and says with her hand covering her mouth*). Ah, yes—we might have saved ourselves the trouble.

MRS. ELVSTED. Did you get a little sleep after that?

HEDDA. Oh, yes. I feel as if I slept pretty well. Didn't you?

MRS. ELVSTED. Not a moment. I couldn't, Hedda. It was absolutely impossible for me.

HEDDA (*rising and going towards her*). There, there, there! There's nothing to worry yourself about. I can see very clearly how it all fits together.

MRS. ELVSTED. Well, what do you think? Can you tell me that?

HEDDA. Why, they naturally kept it up till all hours at Brack's place—

MRS. ELVSTED. Yes, yes—they must have done that. But just the same—

HEDDA. And then, you see, Tesman didn't want to come home and make a fuss and ring the bell in the middle of the night. (*Laughing.*) Perhaps he didn't want to show himself either—so soon after a gay party.

MRS. ELVSTED. But, dear—then where would he go?

HEDDA. Naturally, he's gone to his aunts' and laid him down to sleep there. They keep his old room ready for him.

MRS. ELVSTED. No, he can't be with them. Because just now he got a letter from Miss Tesman. There it is.

HEDDA. So? (*Looks at the envelope.*) Why, so it is; it's in Aunt Julle's handwriting. Well, then, he stayed at Mr. Brack's. And Ejlert Lövborg, he is sitting—with vine leaves in his hair, reading his manuscript.

MRS. ELVSTED. Oh, Hedda, you are just saying things you don't believe yourself.

HEDDA. You really are a silly little thing, Thea.

MRS. ELVSTED. Oh, yes, I suppose I am.

HEDDA. And how tired out you look.

MRS. ELVSTED. Yes, I *am* tired out.

HEDDA. Well then, you do exactly as I say. You go into my bedroom and lie down for a little while on the bed.

MRS. ELVSTED. Oh no, no—I couldn't.

HEDDA. Just try it anyway.

MRS. ELVSTED. Yes, but your husband will surely be coming soon. And I want to know immediately—

HEDDA. I'll call you as soon as he comes.

MRS. ELVSTED. Promise me you will, Hedda?

HEDDA. Yes. You can count on that. You go in and sleep until then.

MRS. ELVSTED. Thanks. In that case, I'll try.

She goes off through the back parlor.

HEDDA *goes up to the glass door and draws the curtains. Broad daylight streams into the room. Then she takes a little handglass from the secretary, looks at herself and fixes her hair. Next she goes to the hall door and presses the call-button. In a moment* BERTE *appears at the hall door.*

BERTE. Is there something you want, ma'am?

HEDDA. Yes. Put some wood on the stove. I'm simply freezing.

BERTE. Saints alive—I'll have it warm in a jiffy. (*She rakes the embers together and lays a piece of wood upon them; then stops and listens.*) That was the front doorbell, ma'am.

HEDDA. Well, go open it. I'll tend the fire myself.
BERTE. It'll catch in a minute.

She goes out by the hall door.

HEDDA *kneels on the footrest and lays some more pieces of wood in the stove. After a short pause* JÖRGEN TESMAN *enters from the hall. He looks tired and reasonably sober. He tiptoes towards the archway and is about to slip through the curtains.*

HEDDA (*at the stove, without looking up*). Good morning.
TESMAN (*turns*). Hedda! (*Approaching her.*) But what in the world—you up so early! Eh?
HEDDA. Yes, I got up very early this morning.
TESMAN. And I was sure you were still asleep in bed! Think of that, Hedda!
HEDDA. Don't speak so loud. Mrs. Elvsted is lying down in my room.
TESMAN. Mrs. Elvsted was here all night!
HEDDA. Yes. No one came to take her home.
TESMAN. Right. Nobody did do that.
HEDDA (*closes the door of the stove and rises*). Well, was it so amusing at Mr. Brack's?
TESMAN. Have you been anxious about me, eh?
HEDDA. No, I wouldn't think of such a thing. I just asked whether you found it amusing.
TESMAN. Yes, indeed, oh, yes. —For once it was. — But mostly in the beginning, I thought. That was when Ejlert read me part of his book. We got there more than an hour too early—think of that! And Brack had all sorts of things to attend to. So Ejlert read to me.
HEDDA (*sitting down by the table on the right*). So? Let me hear about—
TESMAN (*sitting on a footstool near the stove*). Oh

Hedda, you can't imagine what a book that is going to be! I think it's one of the most remarkable books ever written. Just imagine!

HEDDA. Yes, yes. I'm not interested in that—

TESMAN. I must admit one thing, Hedda. After he had read—a most unpleasant feeling came over me.

HEDDA. Unpleasant?

TESMAN. I sat there envying Ejlert for being able to write such a book. Think of that, Hedda!

HEDDA. Yes, I am thinking!

TESMAN. And then to think that he—with the talent he has—should be irreclaimable after all.

HEDDA. Don't you mean he has more daring than other people?

TESMAN. No, for goodness sake, he simply can't be moderate in his pleasures, you see.

HEDDA. And what happened—finally?

TESMAN. Well, I think the nearest word to describe it was a bacchanal, Hedda.

HEDDA. Did he have vine leaves in his hair?

TESMAN. Vine leaves? No, I didn't see anything like that. But he made a long, rambling speech about the woman who had inspired him in his work. Yes, that was exactly the way he put it.

HEDDA. Did he give her name?

TESMAN. No, he didn't. But I can't think of anyone it could be but Mrs. Elvsted. See if I'm right!

HEDDA. Well, where did you leave him?

TESMAN. On the way back. We broke up—the last of us, at the same time. And Brack came with us to get a little fresh air. And so, you see, we agreed to take Ejlert home. Yes, because he was carrying a heavier load than he could handle!

HEDDA. I imagine he was.

TESMAN. But now comes the remarkable part of it, Hedda! Or, the distressing part, I ought to say. Ah—

I am almost ashamed—for Ejlert's sake—to tell you—

HEDDA. Well, then, so—?

TESMAN. Well, when we were on the way back, you see, I fell behind the others a little. Only for a few minutes—imagine!

HEDDA. Yes, yes, Good Lord, but—?

TESMAN. And then, as I hurried to catch up with the others—do you know what I found beside the road? Eh?

HEDDA. No, how can I know that!

TESMAN. Don't say a word to anyone, Hedda. Do you hear! Promise me that, for Ejlert's sake. (*Draws a parcel wrapped in paper from his pocket.*) Imagine— I found this.

HEDDA. Isn't that the package he had with him yesterday?

TESMAN. Exactly, this is the whole of his priceless, irreplaceable manuscript! And he had gone and lost it without knowing it was missing. Think of that, Hedda! So distressing—

HEDDA. But why didn't you give the package back to him at once?

TESMAN. Well, I hardly dared to—in the state he was in—

HEDDA. Didn't you tell anyone else that you had found it?

TESMAN. Oh, far from it. I couldn't for Ejlert's sake, you know.

HEDDA. Then there's nobody who knows you have Ejlert Lövborg's manuscript?

TESMAN. No. And nobody must know it either.

HEDDA. What did you talk to him about after that?

TESMAN. I didn't talk to him at all. Because when we got to town he and two or three of the others got away from us. Think of that!

HEDDA. So? They must have taken him home then.

TESMAN. Yes, that's what they must have done. And Brack went his own way, too.

HEDDA. And what have you been up to since then?

TESMAN. Well, some of the others and I went home with one of the fellows and had our morning coffee with him. Or maybe it would be more accurate to call it our night coffee. Eh? But as soon as I've had a little rest—and as soon as I think poor Ejlert has slept it off, I'll take this over to him.

HEDDA (*holding out her hand for the package*). No, —don't let it out of your hands. Not in such a hurry, I mean. First, let me read it.

TESMAN. No, Hedda, my dear, I couldn't, I really couldn't do that.

HEDDA. You couldn't?

TESMAN. No —for just think what a state he'll be in when he wakes up and finds the manuscript missing. Because he hasn't a copy of it, you understand! He said so himself.

HEDDA (*looks searchingly at him*). Can't something like that be rewritten? Done over?

TESMAN. No, I don't think it would work. Because the inspiration, you see—

HEDDA. Yes, yes—I suppose that's so. —(*Lightly.*) Oh, I just remembered, there's a letter for you.

TESMAN. No, really—!

HEDDA (*hands it to him*). It came early this morning.

TESMAN. From Aunt Julle! What can it be about? (*He puts the package on the other footstool, opens the letter, runs his eyes through it and jumps up.*) Oh, Hedda—she writes that poor Aunt Rina is dying!

HEDDA. Well, that was to be expected.

TESMAN. And if I want to see her again, I must hurry. I'll run over there at once.

HEDDA (*suppressing a smile*). Will you run?

TESMAN. Oh, dearest Hedda—if you could persuade yourself to come with me! Just think!

HEDDA (*rises and says wearily, rejecting the idea*). No, no, don't ask me to do something like that. I don't want to look upon sickness and death. Don't make me come in contact with anything so repulsive.

TESMAN. Yes, My Lord, then—! (*Bustling around.*) My hat—? My overcoat—? Oh, in the hall—I just hope that it won't be too late, Hedda? Eh?

HEDDA. Ah, just run then—

BERTE *appears in the hall door.*

BERTE. Mr. Brack is at the door and he wants to know if he can come in.

TESMAN. At such a time! No, I can't possibly talk to him now.

HEDDA. But I can. (*To* BERTE.) Ask Mr. Brack to come in.

(BERTE *goes out.*)

HEDDA (*whispers quickly*). The package, Tesman!

She snatches it up from the stool.

TESMAN. Yes, give it to me!

HEDDA. No, no, I'll keep it till you return.

She goes to the secretary and puts it in the book case. TESMAN *stands in a flurry of haste and cannot get his gloves on.* MR. BRACK *enters from the hall.*

HEDDA (*nodding to him*). Well, you're certainly an early bird.

BRACK. Yes, don't you think so? (*To* TESMAN.) Are you going out too?

TESMAN. Yes, I must go over to my aunts. Imagine, —the sick one, she's dying, poor dear.

BRACK. Good Lord, she is? Then you mustn't let me hold you up. At such a critical time—

TESMAN. Yes, I really must run. —Good-bye! Good-bye!

He hurries out by the hall door.

HEDDA (*approaching*). It seems to have been something more than lively at your party last night, Mr. Brack.

BRACK. So much so that I haven't even had a chance to change, Mrs. Hedda.

HEDDA. You too?

BRACK. As you see. But what has Tesman been telling you about his adventure last night?

HEDDA. Oh, some dull story. Just that they went out and had coffee somewhere.

BRACK. I've already heard about the coffee-party. Ejlert Lövborg wasn't with them I take it?

HEDDA. No, they took him home before that.

BRACK. Tesman too?

HEDDA. No, some of the others, he said.

BRACK (*smiling*). Jörgen Tesman really is a naïve creature, Mrs. Hedda.

HEDDA. Yes, God knows he is. So there is something more to all this?

BRACK. Yes, it's no good pretending there isn't.

HEDDA. Now then! Let's sit down, dear Mr. Brack, so you can tell your story better.

She sits at the left of the table. BRACK sits near her, at the long side of the table.

HEDDA. Now then?

BRACK. I had good grounds for keeping track of my guests—or more precisely some of my guests, last night.

HEDDA. And among them Ejlert Lövborg, perhaps?

BRACK. I grant you—he was.

HEDDA. Now you make me really curious—

BRACK. Do you know where he and some of the others spent the rest of the night, Hedda?

HEDDA. If it is the sort of thing you can talk about, go ahead.

BRACK. Oh, yes, it can be talked about. Well they ended up at a particularly animated party.

HEDDA. Of the lively variety?

BRACK. The very liveliest—

HEDDA. A little more detail, Mr. Brack—

BRACK. Lövborg and the others had had invitations in advance. I knew all about it. But Lövborg had said he wasn't going. Because he's become a new man, as you know.

HEDDA. Up at the Elvsteds', yes. But he went anyway, then?

BRACK. Well, you see, Hedda—unfortunately last night at my place the spirit moved him—

HEDDA. Yes, I hear he was inspired.

BRACK. Inspired to a rather violent degree. Now I think that must have led him to change his mind. We men—we are, unfortunately, not always so firm in our principles as we ought to be.

HEDDA. Oh, I am sure *you* are an exception, Mr. Brack. But Lövborg—

BRACK. Well, short and sweet—in the end he dropped anchor in Miss Diana's establishment.

HEDDA. Miss Diana's?

BRACK. It was Miss Diana that was giving the party. For a select group of her lady friends and admirers.

HEDDA. Does she have red hair?

BRACK. Indeed she does.

HEDDA. A sort of a—singer?

BRACK. Oh yes—she is that, too. And also a mighty huntress—of men. You must have heard tell of her.

Ejlert Lövborg was one of her warmest backers—in his better days.

HEDDA. And what was the end of it all?

BRACK. Something less than amicable, it seems. Miss Diana went from a most tender reception to outright fisticuffs—

HEDDA. With Lövborg?

BRACK. Yes. He accused her or her friends of having stolen something from him. He declared that his wallet had disappeared. And some other things, too. In a word he seems to have created a murderous spectacle.

HEDDA. How did it all turn out?

BRACK. It turned into a regular cock fight, with both ladies and gentlemen participating. Fortunately the police finally got there.

HEDDA. The police too?

BRACK. Yes. But it is going to be a costly party for Ejlert Lövborg, crazy fellow.

HEDDA. So!

BRACK. Apparently he put up violent resistance. Hit one of the policemen on the head and ripped his coat to shreds. So he went off to the station house with the rest of them.

HEDDA. Where did you learn all this?

BRACK. From the police themselves.

HEDDA (*gazing straight before her*). So that's how it turned out. Then he had no vine leaves in his hair.

BRACK. Vine leaves, Hedda?

HEDDA (*altering her tone*). But now tell me, Mr. Brack, what reason did you have to follow and spy on Ejlert Lövborg like that?

BRACK. First, because it can hardly be a trivial matter for me if it comes out in his examination that he came from my place.

HEDDA. Then there will be an investigation?

BRACK. Of course. However, the chips will have to fall where they may. But I felt that, as a family friend, it was my duty to get a full account of his mighty adventure to you and Tesman.

HEDDA. Why was that, Mr. Brack?

BRACK. Why, because I have a shrewd misgiving that he wants to use you as a sort of front.

HEDDA. No, how can you imagine anything like that!

BRACK. Good Lord—we are not blind, Hedda. Just you watch! This Mrs. Elvsted, she won't be in any hurry to leave the city.

HEDDA. Well, if there is anything between the two of them, there are plenty of other places where they can meet.

BRACK. Not a single home. Every decent house will now be closed to Ejlert Lövborg, just as before.

HEDDA. And you mean that mine ought to be too?

BRACK. Yes. I must say that it would be more than embarrassing to me if this fellow were free to come here. If he, as an outsider, as an intruder, should force his way into—

HEDDA. —into the triangle?

BRACK. Exactly. It would be like finding myself without a home.

HEDDA (*looks at him with a smile*). Ah yes—the only cock in the hamper—that is your goal.

BRACK (*nods slowly and lowers his voice*). Yes, that is my goal. And for that goal I will fight—with all the means in my power.

HEDDA (*her smile vanishing*). It seems you're a dangerous person—when it comes to the point.

BRACK. Do you think so?

HEDDA. Yes, I am beginning to think so, now. And I am very happy—that you have no hold over me, in any way.

BRACK (*with an ambiguous laugh*). Well, well, Hedda—you may be right in that. Who knows what I might do one way or another if I had?

HEDDA. No, but come now, Mr. Brack! That is almost as if you were threatening me.

BRACK (*rising*). Far from it! The triangle, you see— it is best when it is constructed and maintained voluntarily.

HEDDA. There I agree with you.

BRACK. Well, now I have said everything I wanted to. And I had better see about getting home again. Good-bye, Hedda.

He goes towards the glass door.

HEDDA (*rising*). Are you going through the garden?

BRACK. Yes, for me it's shorter.

HEDDA. Yes, and it's also a back way.

BRACK. True, true. I have nothing against back ways. At times they can be rather stimulating.

HEDDA. When there is target practice going on, you mean?

BRACK (*in the doorway, laughing to her*). Oh, no one shoots a tame cock in a basket!

HEDDA (*also laughing*). Oh, no, not when there is only one—

Laughing they exchange nods of farewell. He goes. She closes the door behind him.

HEDDA, *now quite serious, stands for a moment looking out. Presently she goes and peeps through the curtain over the archway. Then she goes to the secretary, takes Lövborg's package out of the bookcase and is about to leaf through the pages.* BERTE *is heard speaking loudly in the hall.* HEDDA *turns and listens. Then she hastily locks the package in the drawer and puts the key on the inkstand.*

EJLERT LÖVBORG, *with his overcoat on and his hat in his hand, tears open the hall door. He looks rather disturbed and irritated.*

LÖVBORG (*looking towards the hall*). I tell you I must come in and I will! There now!

He closes the door, turns, sees HEDDA, *steadies himself at once and bows.*

HEDDA (*at the secretary*). Well, Mr. Lövborg, this is rather late to come for Thea.

LÖVBORG. Rather, I come to you at an early hour. I beg your pardon.

HEDDA. How do you know she's still here?

LÖVBORG. They told me at her room that she had been away all night.

HEDDA (*going to the oval table*). Did you notice anything about the people when they said that?

LÖVBORG (*with an inquiring look*). Notice anything about them?

HEDDA. I mean, did it look as if they thought anything about it?

LÖVBORG (*suddenly understanding*). Oh, yes, that is true. I am dragging her down with me! However, I didn't notice anything. —Tesman isn't up yet?

HEDDA. No—I think not—

LÖVBORG. When did he come home?

HEDDA. Very late.

LÖVBORG. Did he tell you anything?

HEDDA. Yes, I learned that it was very gay at Mr. Brack's.

LÖVBORG. Nothing else?

HEDDA. No, I don't think so. However, I was so very sleepy—

MRS. ELVSTED *enters through the curtains of the archway.*

MRS. ELVSTED (*going towards him*). Ah, Lövborg! At last—!

LÖVBORG. Yes, at last. And too late!

MRS. ELVSTED (*looks at him anxiously*). What is too late?

LÖVBORG. Everything is too late now. I am finished.

MRS. ELVSTED. Oh, no, no—don't say such things.

LÖVBORG. You'll say so yourself when you hear—

MRS. ELVSTED. I won't hear anything!

HEDDA. Perhaps you would rather talk to her alone? If so, I'll leave.

LÖVBORG. No, stay—you, too. Please stay.

MRS. ELVSTED. Yes, but I won't hear anything, I tell you!

LÖVBORG. It's not last night's adventures that I want to talk about.

MRS. ELVSTED. What is it then—?

LÖVBORG. It's this: our ways must part, now.

MRS. ELVSTED. Part!

HEDDA (*involuntarily*). I knew it!

LÖVBORG. Because I have no more use for you, Thea.

MRS. ELVSTED. You can stand there and say that! No more use for me! I can be as much help to you now as I ever was. Won't we go on working together?

LÖVBORG. I don't intend to do any more work.

MRS. ELVSTED (*despairingly*). What am I to do with my life, then?

LÖVBORG. You must try to live your life as if you had never known me.

MRS. ELVSTED. But that is impossible!

LÖVBORG. See if you can, Thea. You must go home again—

MRS. ELVSTED (*in vehement protest*). Never in this world! Where you are, there I will be too! I won't let myself be driven away like this! I'll stay here! To be with you when the book comes out.

HEDDA (*half aloud, in suspense*). Ah, the book—yes!

LÖVBORG (*looks at her*). My book, mine and Thea's. Because it is just *that*.

MRS. ELVSTED. Yes, I feel that way about it. And that's why I have a right to be with you when it comes out! I will be able to see you clothed with respect and honor once more. And the joy, the joy that I will share with you.

LÖVBORG. Thea, our book will never come out.

HEDDA. Ah!

MRS. ELVSTED. Never come out.

LÖVBORG. It never can.

MRS. ELVSTED (*in agonized foreboding*). Lövborg—what have you done with the manuscript?

HEDDA (*looks anxiously at him*). Yes, the manuscript—?

MRS. ELVSTED. Where is it!

LÖVBORG. Oh, Thea—better not ask me about it.

MRS. ELVSTED. Yes, yes, I want to know. I have a right to be told at once.

LÖVBORG. The manuscript. —Well, the—the manuscript, I have torn it into a thousand pieces.

MRS. ELVSTED (*shrieks*). Oh, no, no—!

HEDDA (*involuntarily*). But that's not—

LÖVBORG (*looks at her*). Not true, you think!

HEDDA (*collecting herself*). Oh well, of course. Since you say so yourself. But it sounded so preposterous—

LÖVBORG. True, nevertheless.

MRS. ELVSTED (*wringing her hands*). Oh God—oh God, Hedda—torn his own work to pieces!

LÖVBORG. I have torn my own life to pieces. So why shouldn't I tear up my life work, too—?

MRS. ELVSTED. And you did this last night!

LÖVBORG. Yes, I tell you! Into a thousand pieces. And scattered them on the fjord. Far out. There at least there is clean sea water. Let them drift in it.

Drift with the wind and the current. And after a
while they will sink. Deeper and deeper. Like me,
Thea.

Mrs. ELVSTED. You know what, Lövborg, this business with the manuscript. —All my days it will be to
me as if you had killed a little child.

LÖVBORG. You are right in that. It is a kind of
infanticide.

Mrs. ELVSTED. But how could you, then—! After
all, I had my part in the child, too.

HEDDA (*almost inaudibly*). Ah, the child—

Mrs. ELVSTED (*breathing heavily*). So it is finished.
Well, well, now I'll go, Hedda.

HEDDA. But you're not going to go away?

Mrs. ELVSTED. Oh, I don't know myself what I
shall do. There is nothing before me but the dark.

She goes out by the hall door.

HEDDA (*stands waiting for a moment*). So you are
not going to take her home, Mr. Lövborg?

LÖVBORG. I? Through the streets? Suppose people
were to see her walking with me?

HEDDA. Of course I don't know what else happened
to you last night. But is it so completely beyond repair?

LÖVBORG. It will not end with last night. I know
that perfectly well. But the thing is, now I have no
desire to live that way either. I don't want to begin
it again. It is my courage and my defiance that she
has broken in me.

HEDDA (*looking straight before her*). So that pretty
little fool has had her fingers in a man's fate. (*Looks
at him.*) But how could you be so heartless with her,
even so?

LÖVBORG. Oh, don't call it heartless!

HEDDA. To go and destroy what has occupied her
for a long, long time! That you do not call heartless!

LÖVBORG. Can I speak the truth to you, Hedda?

HEDDA. The truth?

LÖVBORG. First promise me—give me your word that what I am going to tell you, Thea shall never know.

HEDDA. You have my word for that.

LÖVBORG. Good. Then I'll tell you that all that wasn't true, the story I told.

HEDDA. About the manuscript?

LÖVBORG. Yes. I did not tear it to pieces. Or throw it in the fjord, either.

HEDDA. No, no. —But—where is it then?

LÖVBORG. I have destroyed it just the same. Lock, stock, and barrel, Hedda!

HEDDA. This I don't understand.

LÖVBORG. Thea said that what I did seemed like a child murder to her.

HEDDA. Yes—so she said.

LÖVBORG. But to kill his child—that is not the worst thing a father can do.

HEDDA. That is not the worst?

LÖVBORG. No. It was something worse I wanted to spare Thea from hearing.

HEDDA. And what is worse then?

LÖVBORG. Just suppose, Hedda, that a man—in the small hours of the morning—after a wild night of debauchery, came home to the mother of his child and said: "Listen—I have been here and there. This place and that. And I had our child with me. This place and that. And the child got separated from me. Separated completely. The devil knows into whose hand it's fallen. Who's had his fingers on it."

HEDDA. Well—but when all is said and done, this—was only a book—

LÖVBORG. Thea's whole soul was in that book.

HEDDA. Yes, I gather that.

LÖVBORG. And so you can see, there is no future together for her and me.

HEDDA. And what way do you mean to go, then?

LÖVBORG. None. Only try to make an end of the whole thing. The sooner the better.

HEDDA (*a step nearer to him*). Ejlert Lövborg— listen to me. —Won't you try to—to do it beautifully?

LÖVBORG. Beautifully? (*Smiling.*) With vine leaves in my hair, as you used to imagine in the old days—?

HEDDA. Ah, no. Vine leaves—I don't believe in that any more. But beautifully, just the same! For once. —Good-bye! You must go now. And not come here any more.

LÖVBORG. Good-bye, Mrs. Tesman. And remember me to Jörgen Tesman.

He is about to go.

HEDDA. No, wait! You must take a keepsake with you.

She goes to the secretary and opens the drawer and the pistol case. Then she returns to LÖVBORG *with one of the pistols.*

LÖVBORG (*looks at her*). What's *this?* Is *this* the keepsake?

HEDDA (*nodding slowly*). Can you recognize it? Once that was aimed at you.

LÖVBORG. You should have used it then.

HEDDA. There it is! *You* use it now.

LÖVBORG (*puts the pistol in his breast pocket*). Thanks!

HEDDA. And beautifully, Ejlert Lövborg. Promise me that!

LÖVBORG. Good-bye, Hedda Gabler.

He goes out by the hall door. HEDDA *listens for a moment at the door. Then she goes up to the secretary, takes out the package of manuscript, peeps under the cover, draws out a few of the pages and looks at them. Next she goes over and sits in the armchair beside the stove, with the package in her lap. After a moment, she opens the stove door. Then she opens the package.*

HEDDA (*throws some of the leaves into the fire and whispers to herself*). Now I am burning your child, Thea! —You with the curly hair! (*Throwing more leaves into the stove.*) Your child and Ejlert Lövborg's. (*Throws the rest in.*) Now I am burning it—now I am burning your child.

Act Four

The same rooms at the TESMANS'. *It is evening. The front room is in darkness. The back parlor is lighted by the hanging lamp over the table. The curtains over the glass door are closed.*

HEDDA, *dressed in black, walks back and forth in the dark room. Then she goes into the back parlor and disappears to the left. She is heard to strike a few chords on the piano. Presently she comes in sight again and returns to the front room.*

BERTE *enters from the right, through the back parlor, with a lighted lamp, which she places on the table before the corner settee in the front room. Her eyes are red with weeping, and she has mourning ribbons in her cap. She goes quietly and circumspectly out to the right.*

HEDDA *goes up to the glass door, draws the curtain aside a little and looks out into the darkness.*

Shortly afterwards MISS TESMAN, *wearing a mourning hat and veil, comes in from the hall.* HEDDA *goes towards her and holds out her hand.*

MISS TESMAN. Yes, Hedda, here I am, in mourning. The struggle is finally over for my poor sister.

HEDDA. I know already, as you see. Tesman sent a note over to me.

MISS TESMAN. Yes, he promised me that. But I thought after all that to Hedda—here in the house where life is—here I ought to bring the message of death myself.

HEDDA. It was very kind of you.

Miss Tesman. Ah, Rina should not have gone away just *now*. Hedda's home should not be sad at such a time.

Hedda (*changing the subject*). She died very peacefully, Miss Tesman?

Miss Tesman. Oh, it was so beautiful—so peaceful, the release for her. And then the great happiness of seeing Jörgen once more. And bidding him a proper good-bye. —Perhaps he hasn't come home yet?

Hedda. No. He wrote that I shouldn't expect him immediately. But please sit down.

Miss Tesman. No, thank you, you dear—blessed Hedda. I'd like to. But I have so little time. Right now I must dress her and fix her as best I can. She must be tidy when she goes to her grave.

Hedda. Can't I help you with something?

Miss Tesman. Oh, don't think of it! Such things are not for Hedda Tesman to do. Or to think about either. —Not just now. No.

Hedda. Ah, thoughts—they will not always submit to a master—

Miss Tesman (*continuing*). Yes, Lord, that's the way the world goes. At home we shall be sewing linen for Rina. And here there will also be sewing soon, I think. But that will be another sort, that will—God be praised!

Jörgen Tesman *enters by the hall door.*

Hedda. Ah, it's a good thing you've finally got back.

Tesman. Are you here Aunt Julle? With Hedda? Think of that!

Miss Tesman. I was just about to go, my dear boy. Now, did you take care of the things you promised me?

Tesman. No—I'm really afraid I've forgotten half of them, you see. I must come over to see you again tomorrow. Today my head is completely confused. I can't keep my thoughts in line.

MISS TESMAN. Why, Jörgen dear, you mustn't take it like this.

TESMAN. No? What do you mean?

MISS TESMAN. You should be glad in your sorrow. Glad about what has just happened. The way I am.

TESMAN. Oh, yes, yes. You are thinking of Aunt Rina, aren't you?

HEDDA. It will be very lonely for you now, Miss Tesman.

MISS TESMAN. In the first days, yes. But that won't last very long, I hope. My blessed Rina's little room won't stay empty, I'm sure!

TESMAN. So? Who do you expect to move into it? Eh?

MISS TESMAN. Oh, there's always some poor invalid or other who needs care and nursing, unfortunately.

HEDDA. Do you really want to take such a cross on you again?

MISS TESMAN. A cross! God forgive you, child—that wasn't the least bit of a cross for me.

HEDDA. But if you are going to take in a complete stranger who——

MISS TESMAN. Oh, you quickly make friends with sick people. And I need so much to have someone to live for, me too. Well God be praised and thanked— here in this house there may also be one thing or another where an old aunt may make herself useful.

HEDDA. Don't count on anything here.

TESMAN. Yes, just imagine how nice a time we three could have together if—

HEDDA. If——?

TESMAN (uneasily). Oh, nothing. It will come out all right. Let's hope it will. What?

MISS TESMAN. Yes, yes. You two have something

to chat about, I imagine. (*Smiling.*) And perhaps Hedda has something to tell you, too, Jörgen. Good-bye! Now, I must go home to Rina. (*Turning at the door.*) Lord, how queer it is to think of. Now Rina is with me and with blessed Jochum at the same time.

TESMAN. Yes, imagine that, Aunt Julle! What?

MISS TESMAN *goes out by the hall door.*

HEDDA (*cold and searching, follows* TESMAN *with her eyes*). I almost believe the death is more grief to you than to her.

TESMAN. Oh, it's not just the death. It's Ejlert I'm all upset about.

HEDDA (*quickly*). Is there something new about him?

TESMAN. I ran up to his place this afternoon to tell him his manuscript was in good hands.

HEDDA. Well, didn't you find him?

TESMAN. No. He wasn't home. But afterwards I met Mrs. Elvsted and she said he'd been here early this morning.

HEDDA. Yes, just after you left.

TESMAN. And he seems to have said that he had torn his manuscript to pieces. What?

HEDDA. Yes, he insisted he had.

TESMAN. But, good heavens, he must have been completely out of his mind! So I guess you didn't dare give it back to him, Hedda?

HEDDA. No, he didn't get it.

TESMAN. But of course you told him that we had it?

HEDDA. No. (*Quickly.*) Did you tell Mrs. Elvsted by any chance?

TESMAN. No, I didn't want to. But you ought to have told Ejlert himself. Imagine if he went off in despair and did himself some harm! Let me take the manuscript, Hedda! I will run over to him with it now. Where is the package?

HEDDA (*cold and immovable, leaning against the armchair*). I don't have it any more.

TESMAN. Don't have it? What on earth do you mean by that?

HEDDA. I burned it up—every bit.

TESMAN (*with a violent start of terror*). Burned it! Burned Ejlert's manuscript!

HEDDA. Don't scream like that. The maid might hear you.

TESMAN. Burned! But, Good God—! No, no, no—this is impossible!

HEDDA. Yes, but it is so, just the same.

TESMAN. But, just realize what you have done, Hedda! It's unlawful treatment of lost property. Imagine that! Yes, ask Mr. Brack. He's a lawyer; he'll tell you.

HEDDA. My advice to you is not to say anything about it—to Mr. Brack or anybody else.

[handwritten margin note: LEGAL ASPECT]

TESMAN. But how could you go and do anything so unheard of! How could it have entered your mind? What came over you? Tell me that. Eh?

HEDDA (*suppressing an almost imperceptible smile*). I did it for you, Jörgen.

TESMAN. For me?

HEDDA. When you came home this morning and told me that he had read to you—

TESMAN. Yes, yes, what then?

HEDDA. You admitted then that you envied him the work.

TESMAN. Oh, Good Lord, I didn't mean literally.

HEDDA. Just the same. I couldn't bear the thought that anyone else should put you in the shade.

TESMAN (*bursting out, between doubt and joy*). Hedda! Oh, is this true, what you just said? —But—

but—I never thought your love was as strong as that. Just imagine!

HEDDA. Well, it's best that you should know—that just now —(*Impatiently breaking off.*) No, no—you can go ask Aunt Julle. She'll give you the information.

TESMAN. Oh, I almost believe I understand you, Hedda! (*Clasps his hands together.*) No, Good Lord, you—can it be *that!* Eh?

HEDDA. Don't shout so. The maid can hear.

TESMAN (*laughing in irrepressible glee*). The maid! No, you really are priceless, Hedda! The maid—it's only Berte! I'll go tell Berte myself.

HEDDA (*clenching her hands together in desperation*). Oh, it will kill me—it will kill me, all this!

TESMAN. What will, Hedda? Eh?

HEDDA (*coldly, controlling herself*). All this—nonsense—Jörgen.

TESMAN. Nonsense? That I am so overjoyed? But after all—perhaps I had better not say anything to Berte.

HEDDA. Oh, yes—why not that, too?

TESMAN. No, no, not just now! But Aunt Julle must certainly be told. And also that you've begun to call me Jörgen! Think of it! Oh, Aunt Julle'll—

HEDDA. When she hears I burned Ejlert Lövborg's manuscript—for you?

TESMAN. No, now that I think of it, that business about the manuscript—nobody must know about that of course. But that you are warming up towards me, Hedda—Aunt Julle must certainly share in that! Further, I am curious to know if such a thing is common with young wives? What?

HEDDA. You must ask Aunt Julle about *that,* too, I think.

TESMAN. Yes, I will certainly do that when I get a

chance. (*Looks uneasy and downcast again.*) And yet—and yet, the manuscript, Good God! It's terrible to think about poor Ejlert, just the same.

MRS. ELVSTED, *dressed as in the first act, with hat and coat, enters by the hall door.*

MRS. ELVSTED (*greets them hurriedly and speaks in evident agitation*). Oh, dear Hedda, don't be annoyed because I have come back.

HEDDA. What's the matter with you, Thea?

TESMAN. Is it something to do with Ejlert Lövborg again—Eh?

MRS. ELVSTED. Yes! I am so dreadfully afraid he has had some kind of accident.

HEDDA (*seizes her arm*). Ah—you think so!

TESMAN. Why, but Good Lord—what makes you think such a thing, Mrs. Elvsted?

MRS. ELVSTED. Yes. Because I heard them talking at the pension—just as I came in. Oh, the most incredible rumors are going around today about him.

TESMAN. Yes, imagine, I heard something too! And yet I can swear he went straight home to bed! Imagine that!

HEDDA. Well—what were they saying at the pension?

MRS. ELVSTED. Oh, I didn't catch anything definite. Either they didn't know very much, or else. —They stopped talking when they saw me. And as for making inquiries—I didn't dare.

TESMAN (*moving about uneasily*). We must hope— we must hope that you heard wrong, Mrs. Elvsted.

MRS. ELVSTED. No, no—I know he was the one they were talking about. And as I heard it, there was some mention of a hospital or—

TESMAN. A hospital!

HEDDA. No—surely that's impossible!

MRS. ELVSTED. Oh, I was mortally afraid for him!

And so I went to his lodgings and asked about him there.

HEDDA. *Could* you bring yourself to that, Thea?

MRS. ELVSTED. Yes. What else could I do? For I didn't think I could stand not to know another minute.

TESMAN. But you didn't find him there either? What?

MRS. ELVSTED. No. And the people didn't know anything about him. He hadn't been home since yesterday afternoon, they said.

TESMAN. Yesterday! Imagine saying that!

MRS. ELVSTED. Oh, I think the only possible thing is that something terrible has happened to him!

TESMAN. Hedda dear—if I went over, what do you think, and made inquiries in various places—?

HEDDA. No, no—don't you get mixed up in this.

MR. BRACK, *with his hat in his hand, enters by the hall door, which* BERTE *opens and closes behind him. He looks grave and bows in silence.*

TESMAN. Oh, is that you, Brack? Eh?

BRACK. Yes. I had to see you this evening.

TESMAN. I can see you have heard the news from Aunt Julle.

BRACK. I have also heard that, yes.

TESMAN. Isn't it sad? Eh?

BRACK. Well, my dear Tesman, that depends on how you look at it.

TESMAN (*looks dubiously at him*). Has anything else happened?

BRACK. Yes, indeed it has.

HEDDA (*in suspense*). Something sad, Mr. Brack?

BRACK. Also . . . how you look at it, Mrs. Tesman.

MRS. ELVSTED (*unable to restrain her anxiety*). Oh, it's something to do with Ejlert Lövborg!

BRACK (*with a glance at her*). How did you happen

to stumble on *that,* Madame? Perhaps you already
knew something—?

MRS. ELVSTED (*in confusion*). No, no, I didn't at
all; but—

TESMAN. But for heaven's sake, tell us!

BRACK (*shrugging his shoulders*). Well—unfortunately—Ejlert Lövborg has been taken to the hospital. He's at the point of death.

MRS. ELVSTED (*shrieks*). Oh, God! Oh, God—!

TESMAN. To the hospital! And at the point of death.

HEDDA (*involuntarily*). So quickly then—

MRS. ELVSTED (*wailing*). And we parted without
making up, Hedda!

HEDDA (*whispers*). But Thea—careful, Thea!

MRS. ELVSTED (*not heeding her*). I must go to him!
I must see him alive!

BRACK. It will be of no use, Madame. They permit
no one to see him.

MRS. ELVSTED. Oh, but at least tell me what happened to him? What is it?

TESMAN. Yes, because he didn't—himself—! Eh?

HEDDA. Oh, but I am sure he did.

TESMAN. Hedda—how can you—?

BRACK (*keeping his eyes fixed on* HEDDA). You have
unfortunately guessed quite right, Mrs. Tesman.

MRS. ELVSTED. Oh, how dreadful!

TESMAN. Himself, then! Think of that!

HEDDA. Shot himself!

BRACK. Also rightly guessed, Mrs. Tesman.

MRS. ELVSTED (*with an effort at self-control*). When
did it happen, Mr. Brack?

BRACK. This afternoon. Between three and four.

TESMAN. But Good Lord—then where did he do
it? Eh?

BRACK (*with some hesitation*). Where? Well—he
must have done it at his lodgings.

MRS. ELVSTED. No, that can't be right. Because I was there between six and seven.

BRACK. Well, some other place then. I don't know precisely. I only know he was found. —He had shot himself—in the breast.

MRS. ELVSTED. Oh, how terrible to think of. That he should end like that!

HEDDA (*to* BRACK). Was it in the breast?

BRACK. Yes—as I said.

HEDDA. Not in the temple? -

BRACK. In the breast, Mrs. Tesman.

HEDDA. Well, well—the breast is a good place, too.

BRACK. How's that, Mrs. Tesman?

HEDDA (*evasively*). Oh, nothing—nothing, really.

TESMAN. And the wound is dangerous, you say? What?

BRACK. The wound is absolutely mortal. Probably it is all over with him already.

MRS. ELVSTED. Yes, yes, I feel it! It is all over! All over! Oh, Hedda—!

TESMAN. But tell me—how did you get to know all this?

BRACK (*curtly*). Through one of the police. A man I had some business with.

HEDDA (*in a clear voice*). At long last—an act!

TESMAN (*terrified*). God bless me—what are you saying Hedda?

HEDDA. I say there is something beautiful in this.

BRACK. Mm, Mrs. Tesman—

TESMAN. Beautiful! No, think of that!

MRS. ELVSTED. Oh, Hedda, how can you talk about beauty in such a thing!

HEDDA. Ejlert Lövborg has closed his own account. He had the courage to do what—what must be done.

MRS. ELVSTED. No, never believe it, that it was like that! What he did was done when he was delirious.

TESMAN. When he was in despair!

HEDDA. He was not. I am sure of that.

MRS. ELVSTED. Oh, but he was! Delirious! Just as when he tore our book to pieces.

BRACK (*surprised*). The book? The manuscript, you mean? He tore that to pieces?

MRS. ELVSTED. Yes, he did it last night.

TESMAN (*whispers softly*). Oh, Hedda, we shall never escape from this.

BRACK. Mm, that's strange.

TESMAN (*moving about the room*). Just to think of Ejlert going out of the world in such a way! And not even leaving behind him the work that would have made his name enduring—

MRS. ELVSTED. Oh, if it could only be put together again!

TESMAN. Yes, think, if it only could! I don't know what I wouldn't give—

MRS. ELVSTED. Perhaps it could, Mr. Tesman.

TESMAN. What do you mean?

MRS. ELVSTED (*searches in the pocket of her dress*). Look here. I have kept all the loose notes he had with him when he dictated.

HEDDA (*steps forward*). Ah—!

TESMAN. You kept them, Mrs. Elvsted! Eh?

MRS. ELVSTED. Yes, I have them here. I brought them with me when I set out. And here they still are in my pocket—

TESMAN. Oh, let me just have a look!

MRS. ELVSTED (*hands him a bundle of notes*). But they're all out of order. So mixed up.

TESMAN. Think, if we could straighten them out, just the same! Perhaps if we could work together—

MRS. ELVSTED. Oh, yes, let's try it anyway—

TESMAN. It *will* work! It *must!* I will give my life to it.

HEDDA. You, Jörgen? Your life?

TESMAN. Yes, or rather all the time I can spare. My own collections will have to wait for the time being. Hedda—you understand me, eh? This is something I owe to Ejlert's memory.

HEDDA. Perhaps so.

TESMAN. And so, Mrs. Elvsted, we will pull ourselves together. Lord, it's no good brooding over what's happened. What? We must make our minds as easy as we can, in order—

MRS. ELVSTED. Yes, yes, Mr. Tesman, I'll do my best.

TESMAN. Well then, come over here. We must look over the notes right now. Where shall we sit? Here? No, there, in the back room. Excuse me, Brack. Come with me, Mrs. Elvsted.

MRS. ELVSTED. Oh, God—if only it will work!

TESMAN *and* MRS. ELVSTED *go into the back room. She takes off her hat and cloak. They sit at the table under the hanging lamp and are soon deep in an eager study of the papers.* HEDDA *crosses to the stove and sits in the armchair After a moment,* BRACK *goes up to her.*

HEDDA (*in a low voice*). Oh, Mr. Brack, what a sense of relief there is in this act of Ejlert Lövborg's.

BRACK. Relief, Hedda? Yes, for him it is certainly a relief—

HEDDA. I mean for me. It's a relief to know that there can still be an act of free will and courage in this world. Something that gleams with uncalculated beauty.

BRACK (*smiling*). Mm—my dear Hedda—

HEDDA. Oh, I know what you are going to say. For you are a kind of scholar, too, like—well!

BRACK (*looking hard at her*). Ejlert Lövborg was

more to you than you perhaps will admit to yourself. Or am I making a mistake?

HEDDA. I won't answer such a question. I only know that Ejlert Lövborg has had the courage to act out his life in his own way. And now—the greatest gesture! This, with its beauty. This, that he had the strength and the will to turn away from the banquet of life—so early.

BRACK. It pains me, Hedda—but I must destroy this pretty make believe of yours.

HEDDA. Make believe?

BRACK. Which would have been destroyed very soon anyway.

HEDDA. And what is it, then?

BRACK. He did not shoot himself—of his own will.

HEDDA. Not of his own will!

BRACK. No. The story of Ejlert Lövborg did not occur quite as I told it.

HEDDA (*in suspense*). Have you concealed something? What is it?

BRACK. I did alter a few small details for the sake of poor Mrs. Elvsted.

HEDDA. And they were—?

BRACK. First, that he is actually dead already.

HEDDA. In the hospital?

BRACK. Yes. And without coming to.

HEDDA. What else did you conceal?

BRACK. This—the thing did not take place in his lodgings.

HEDDA. Oh, that can hardly make much difference.

BRACK. But perhaps it may. Because I should tell you—Ejlert Lövborg was found shot in—in Miss Diana's boudoir.

HEDDA (*starting to spring up, then sinking back*). That is impossible, Mr. Brack! He can't have been *there* again today.

BRACK. He was there this afternoon. He came there to ask for something, as he put it, they had taken from him. Talked wildly about a child that had been lost—

HEDDA. Ah—that's why—

BRACK. I thought that perhaps he meant his manuscript. But now I hear he destroyed it himself. So I suppose it must have been his wallet.

HEDDA. It must have been. And there—there he was found?

BRACK. Yes, there. With a discharged pistol in his breast pocket. The shot had given him a mortal wound.

HEDDA. In the breast—yes.

BRACK. No—it struck him in the belly.

HEDDA (*looks up at him with an expression of loathing*). That, too! Oh, ludicrousness and meanness lies like a curse on everything I so much as touch.

BRACK. There is still another thing, Hedda. Another thing that also comes under the heading of "mean."

HEDDA. And what is that?

BRACK. The pistol he had with him—

HEDDA (*breathless*). So! What of that!

BRACK. He must have stolen it.

HEDDA (*leaps up*). Stolen it! That is not true! That he did not do!

BRACK. There's no other possibility. He *must* have stolen it. —Hush!

TESMAN *and* MRS. ELVSTED *get up from the table in the back parlor and come into the living room.*

TESMAN (*with the papers in both his hands*). Hedda dear—it's next to impossible to see in there under that lamp. Think of that!

HEDDA. Yes, I am thinking.

TESMAN. Perhaps it will be all right if we sit at your secretary for a little while. What?

HEDDA. Yes, I don't mind. (*Quickly.*) No, wait! Let me clean it off first!

TESMAN. Oh, there's no need of that, Hedda. There's enough room.

HEDDA. No, no, let me clean it off, I say! I'll take these things in and put them on the piano. There.

She has drawn out an object, covered with a sheet of music, from under the bookcase, places several other pieces of music on it and carries the whole into the back parlor to the left. TESMAN lays the scraps of paper on the secretary and moves the lamp there from the corner table. He and MRS. ELVSTED sit down and fall to working. HEDDA comes back in.

HEDDA (*behind* MRS. ELVSTED's *chair, gently ruffling her hair*). Well, my sweet Thea—how goes it with Ejlert Lövborg's memorial?

MRS. ELVSTED (*looks dispiritedly up at her*). Oh, Lord. —It seems like a tremendous job to straighten it out.

TESMAN. It *must* be done. That's all there is to it. And this sort of thing, setting other men's papers to rights—this is just the sort of thing I am best at.

HEDDA goes over to the stove and sits on one of the footstools. BRACK stands over her, leaning against the armchair.

HEDDA (*whispers*). What was that you said about the pistol?

BRACK (*softly*). That he must have stolen it.

HEDDA. Why stolen it?

BRACK. Because every other explanation ought to be impossible, Hedda.

HEDDA. So?

BRACK (*glances at her*). Ejlert Lövborg was here this morning, of course. Was he not?

HEDDA. Yes.

BRACK. Were you alone with him?

HEDDA. Yes, part of the time.

BRACK. Didn't you leave the room while he was here?

HEDDA. No.

BRACK. Try to remember. Weren't you ever out a moment?

HEDDA. Well, yes, perhaps for just a moment—out in the hall.

BRACK. And where was your pistol case during that time?

HEDDA. I had it in—

BRACK. Well, Hedda?

HEDDA. The case was there in the secretary.

BRACK. Have you looked since, to see whether both pistols are there?

HEDDA. No.

BRACK. Well, you don't need to. I saw the pistol Lövborg had with him. And I recognized it at once from yesterday. And from before yesterday, too.

HEDDA. Have you got it with you?

BRACK. No. The police have it.

HEDDA. What will the police do with the pistol?

BRACK. Search till they find the owner.

HEDDA. Do you think they can find him?

BRACK (*bends over her and whispers*). No, Hedda Gabler—not so long as I am silent.

HEDDA (*looks at him in fright*). And if you aren't silent—then what?

BRACK (*shrugs his shoulders*). There is always another way—say that the pistol was stolen.

HEDDA (*firmly*). Rather death!

BRACK (*smiling*). People *say* such things. But they don't *do* them.

HEDDA (*without replying*). And supposing the pistol was not stolen. And the owner is discovered. What comes next?

BRACK. Well, Hedda—then comes the scandal.

HEDDA. The scandal!

BRACK. The scandal, yes—which you are so terribly afraid of. You will, of course, be brought into court. Both you and Miss Diana. She will have to explain how the thing happened. Whether it was accident or murder. Did he try to take the pistol out of his pocket to shoot her? And it went off then? Or did she grab the pistol out of his hand, shoot him, and stick it back in his pocket again? That would be like her. Because she's a hefty wench, this same Miss Diana.

HEDDA. But all these disgusting things have nothing to do with *me*.

BRACK. No. But you will have to answer the question: Why did you give Ejlert Lövborg the pistol? And what conclusions will people draw from the fact that you did give it to him?

HEDDA (*lets her head sink*). That is true. I didn't think of that.

BRACK. Still, fortunately, there is no danger, so long as I am silent.

HEDDA (*looks up at him*). So I am in your power, Mr. Brack. You have me, neck and hand, from now on.

BRACK (*whispers softly*). Dearest Hedda—believe me—I shall not misuse my position.

HEDDA. In your power, just the same. Subject to your will and your demands. A slave, a slave then! (*Rises impetuously.*) No—I can't stand the thought of such a thing! Never!

BRACK (*looks half-mockingly at her*). People usually learn to put up with the inevitable.

HEDDA (*returns his look*). Yes, perhaps. (*She crosses to the secretary. Suppressing an involuntary smile, she imitates* TESMAN's *intonations.*) Well? Does your work prosper, Jörgen? What?

TESMAN. Heaven knows, dear. In any case there's a good many months' work in this job.

HEDDA (*as before*). No, imagine that! (*Passes her hands softly through* MRS. ELVSTED's *hair.*) Doesn't it seem strange to you, Thea? Now you are sitting here with Tesman—just as you used to sit with Ejlert Lövborg?

MRS. ELVSTED. Ah, if I could only inspire your husband, too.

HEDDA. Oh, that will come, all right—in time

TESMAN. Yes, you know, Hedda—I really think I begin to feel something of the sort. But you go over there and sit with Brack again.

HEDDA. Isn't there anything I can do to help you two?

TESMAN. No, nothing in the world. (*Turning his head.*) For the time being will you be good enough to keep Hedda company, my dear Brack?

BRACK (*with a glance at* HEDDA). It will give me the greatest pleasure.

HEDDA. Thanks. But tonight I am tired. I'll lie down on the sofa in there for a bit.

TESMAN. Yes, do that, dear. What?

HEDDA *goes into the back parlor and draws the curtains. A short pause. Suddenly she is heard playing a wild dance tune on the piano.*

MRS. ELVSTED (*starts from her chair*). Oh—what is that!

TESMAN (*runs to the archway*). But, my dearest Hedda—don't play dance music tonight! Remember Aunt Rina! And Ejlert, too!

HEDDA (*puts her head out between the curtains*). And Aunt Julle. And all the rest. —After this, I will be quiet.

Closes the curtains again.

TESMAN (*at the writing table*). It isn't good for her to see us at this sad work. I'll tell you what, Mrs. Elvsted—you take the empty room at Aunt Julle's. I will come over there evenings. And we can sit and work there. What?

MRS. ELVSTED. Yes, that might be the best way—

HEDDA (*in the inner room*). I heard very clearly what you said, Tesman. But how am I to get through the evenings out here?

TESMAN (*turning over the papers*). Oh, Mr. Brack will be kind enough to come out and see you now and then.

BRACK (*in the armchair, calls out gaily*). Gladly. Every single evening, Mrs. Tesman! We'll have a fine time together here, we two!

HEDDA (*speaking loud and clear*). Yes, that's closer to what you've been hoping for, Brack? You, as the only cock in the basket—

A shot is heard within. TESMAN, MRS. ELVSTED *and* BRACK *leap to their feet.*

TESMAN. Oh, now she is playing with the pistols again.

He throws back the curtains and runs in, followed by MRS. ELVSTED. HEDDA *lies stretched on the sofa, lifeless. Confusion and cries.* BERTE *enters in alarm from the right.*

TESMAN (*shrieks to* BRACK). Shot herself! Shot herself in the temple. Imagine that!

BRACK (*half-fainting in the armchair*). But God pity us—such things simply are *not* done.

BIBLIOGRAPHY

LIFE

Koht, Halvdan, *The Life of Henrik Ibsen.* London, Allen and Unwin, 1931.

Morrison, Mary, ed., *The Correspondence of Henrik Ibsen.* London, Hodder and Stoughton, 1905.

Zucker, A. E., *Ibsen, the Master Builder.* New York, Holt, Rinehart and Winston, Inc., 1929.

CRITICISM

Bradbrook, M. C., *Ibsen the Norwegian.* London, Chatto and Windus, 1948.

Downs, Brian, *Ibsen, the Intellectual Background.* Cambridge (Eng.), Cambridge U.P., 1946.

——— *A Study of Six Plays by Ibsen.* Cambridge (Eng.), Cambridge U.P., 1950.

Northam, John, *Ibsen's Dramatic Method.* London, Faber and Faber, 1953.

Shaw, Bernard, *The Quintessence of Ibsenism.* New York, Hill and Wang, n.d.

Tennant, P. F. D., *Ibsen's Dramatic Technique.* Cambridge (Eng.), Bowes and Bowes, 1948.

Weigant, H. J., *The Modern Ibsen.* New York, Holt, Rinehart and Winston, Inc., 1926.